Ed Koch on Everything

ED KOCH
on Everything

*Movies, Politics,
Personalities, Food,
and Other Stuff*

by Edward I. Koch

A Birch Lane Press Book
Published by Carol Publishing Group

A Birch Lane Press Book
Published by Carol Publishing Group
Birch Lane Press is a registered trademark of Carol Communications, Inc.
Editorial Offices: 600 Madison Avenue, New York, N.Y. 10022
Sales and Distribution Offices: 120 Enterprise Avenue, Secaucus, N.J. 07094
In Canada: Canadian Manda Group, P.O. Box 920, Station U, Toronto, Ontario
   M8Z 5P9
Queries regarding rights and permissions should be addressed to Carol
   Publishing Group, 600 Madison Avenue, New York, N.Y. 10022

Carol Publishing Group books are available at special discounts for bulk purchases, for sales promotions, fund-raising, or educational purposes Special editions can be created to specifications. For details, contact Special Sales Department, Carol Publishing Group, 120 Enterprise Avenue, Secaucus, N.J. 07094

Manufactured in the United States of America
10 9 8 7 6 5 4 3 2 1

Library of Congress Cataloging-in-Publication Data

Koch, Ed, 1924–
    Ed Koch on everything : movies, politics, personalities,
food, and other stuff / by Edward I. Koch.
       p.   cm.
    "A Birch Lane Press book."
    ISBN 1-55972-225-8
    1. Popular culture—New York (N.Y.) 2. Popular culture—United
States. 3. New York (N.Y.)—Social life and customs. 4. New York (N.Y.)—
Politics and government—1951– I. Title.
F128.54.K63A25 1994
974.7'1—dc20   93-46037
                                                                      CIP

This book is dedicated to the new generation in my family: Jordan Thaler, eight months, living in New York City, and Kayla Thaler, three years, living in California. They will each make their own mark. Why? Because they are loved and will grow up secure. And don't forget the genes.

Contents

Preface

One of my joys in life is writing. When I was mayor I wrote columns on local issues which were published in weekly newspapers throughout New York City, along with a special, more thoughtful column for the *Staten Island Advance*. Unlike many public officials, I really wrote them. I saw the columns as an opportunity to take my message directly to the public without having it intercepted and interpreted by the media, many of whom subsisted on mayor bashing.

My writing skills were sharpened in Congress, where I learned that the way to raise the consciousness of your colleagues was by inundating them with expertise on particular issues, subjects in which they were interested but about which they had little knowledge. The key was to put your ideas down on paper and get them published in the *Congressional Record*. I knew that few of my fellow members would actually read my statements, but their staffers would, and the members would see my name attached to the headline describing the subject. Quantity in this case came close to quality in impact. If you wrote often enough and exhibited an understanding of the subject, you would be perceived as someone to be looked to for leadership in that area. If your statement was less than three hundred words, it led off that day's *Congressional Record*. Longer pieces were published in the back of the book. Just like riding on a bus, being in the front was worth fighting for.

I know that I placed more statements in the *Congressional Record* than any member of Congress other than Dr. Larry MacDonald, the most right-wing member of Congress at that time. I was representing the left, at least in my mind. After leaving Congress, MacDonald was a victim of the fatal Korean KAL 007 airline explosion over the USSR.

Besides columns, I also wrote and published four books during my twelve years as mayor. My fifth book, *Citizen Koch*, was published in 1992, two years after I left office. My first book, *Mayor*, received a lot of attention because it was unusual for an incumbent mayor to write a candid book on politics. On the day it was published, I held a press conference at City Hall which was hugely attended. As Maurice Chevalier said in *Gigi*, "I remember it well."

A snotty, young woman reporter whom I had never seen before said, "Mayor, why should we believe you wrote this book?" Without blinking, I said to her, "It is easy to convince you. Close your eyes and let me read it aloud to you." I said that because my books have my distinctive voice. I am not an intellectual or a genius but I believe that consistent, thoughtful common sense grounded in a philosophy representing the shared values of the middle class can take the place of brilliance. I've got lots of common sense: Indeed on my daily WABC radio show I refer to myself as the Voice of Reason. I've trademarked the phrase, so I'm the only Voice of Reason in America. My distinctive voice with its New York inflection, common sense, and humor can be heard on each page. Why? Because the book is dictated, not hacked out on a word processor. Talk reads differently from writing and the cadence of a dictated book is distinctive, especially when read aloud.

The material in this book consists of political columns and movie reviews. The political columns, which originally appeared in the *New York Post* and *Daily News*, were dictated. My movie reviews, on the other hand, were written by hand on Sunday mornings while I lay in bed eating my bagel and whitefish salad with onion and tomato. Test it for yourself; read them aloud and you will see what I mean.

I'm particularly proud of my political columns. They not only have a strong point of view on controversial matters reflecting my intensity of feeling, but more times than not they go against the flow of other columns on the same subject by more established writers. Most important, I am not knee jerk in my thoughts. My philosophy can be summed up as a liberal with sanity.

My movie columns are also different in approach. Very often I attack other movie reviewers for giving rave reviews to movies that should only appear on home video.

Let me tell you how I was retained in both instances. When I was leaving the mayor's office, the then publisher of the *New York Post*, Peter Kalikow, and the *Post*'s editorial page editor, Eric Breindel, asked me to write a weekly column for the *Post*. I signed on and wrote for the *Post* until March of 1993. I resigned because of a hostile (and ultimately unsuccessful) takeover bid for the paper by New York real estate developer Abe Hirschfeld. After Hirschfeld fired Eric Breindel and announced that he was bringing in Bill Tatum, editor of the Harlem-based *Amsterdam News*, a crudely anti-white, racist newspaper, I knew I could not continue to write for the *Post*.

After I announced my resignation, I received a call from Mort Zuckerman, the new publisher and owner of the *Daily News*, who hired me. My column appeared in the *News* every Friday until February 1994. In March I resumed writing for the *New York Post*.

My foray into movie criticism came as the result of a telephone call from the publisher and editor of *The Manhattan Spirit*, Tom Allon. He said, "Mayor, I know you like movies. Would you like to write reviews for us?" So I said, "Yes, I like to write and I do like movies. What do you pay?" He said, "Fifty dollars a review." I replied, "I don't cross the street for fifty dollars," not knowing what a fair price would be. He said,

"What would you want?" I gave him the amount. He said that was too much for a small paper to pay. I said, "I understand. Call me back when you get bigger."

They grew overnight, because he called me back the next day and gave me what I asked for. In exchange I gave him permission to run the column in five papers all owned by News Communications Inc.: *The Manhattan Spirit*, *Our Town* (both in Manhattan), *Dan's Papers* (in the Hamptons), *Queens Tribune*, *Bronx Times Reporter*, and *Bronx Press Review*.

I announced the first week that I would review differently than most reviewers. There would be no rating system with gradations using stars or other symbols. The movie would get either a plus or a minus. Either I liked it or I didn't. I have been consistent, even when I knew that I would be perceived as a Philistine when I gave *Howard's End*, a beautifully boring film, a minus. I did the same thing to *The Piano*.

My reviews are basically for people who go to the movies for pleasure. I don't have the expertise or inclination to compare Bergman with Bunuel, or comment on the cinematography or other refinements. I simply let readers know if a particular film will be two hours well spent. It's gratifying to go to the movies and be told by many fellow moviegoers that they approve of the approach.

When published, my political column runs approximately 750 words. I use the weekends to mull over an appropriate subject for the column. This is the most difficult and often painful part of the process: coming up with a new approach to a subject. Rarely is a column by anyone, no matter how gifted, the first discussion of the subject. Then on Monday I dictate my first draft, which is usually over a thousand words. Now I will reveal the process which in cooking is called reduction.

My staff includes my executive assistant, Rosemarie Connors-McCallion, who, while our DNA is different, thinks like I do. Each week she edits the column with Dan Wolf, an old friend and now my editor, who was the founding editor of the *Village Voice*. They go over every line making editorial changes, never altering the substance of my thoughts, but clarifying and reducing my overwrite to the proper length.

When they have done that truly amazing job, I then—and here I think the approach is unique—vet the columns by sending them to a group of friends for their criticism and suggestions. That editing team has included Jim Gill, my law partner at Robinson Silverman Pearce Aronsohn and Berman; New York City Parks Commissioner Henry Stern, then president of the Citizens Union; the late Robert Wagner, Jr., Vice Chairman of LH Research and former Deputy Mayor; Allen Schwartz, lawyer and former Corporation Counsel (when he recently became a U.S. District Court judge he was removed from the list of vetters); Abe Biderman, Chief Financial Officer with Lipper & Company and former Finance Commissioner; Jonathan R. Cohen, Director of Public Policy for Joseph E. Seagram & Sons, Inc., and former advisor to the mayor; and Clifford Chanin, Associate Director for Arts and Humanities at the Rockefeller Foundation and former assistant press secretary.

I want it clearly understood that I come up with the ideas for the columns myself, write all the first drafts, and then work on the column through each stage of editing. All changes are approved by me and I often alter the proposed changes to comport with my idiosyncratic thinking.

My movie columns are not sent to the editing team, but to those people with whom I've seen the film. They then have the opportunity to give me a sentence or two which I insert at the end of the review giving their opinions, sometimes not in accord with mine. I identify them only by initials, but you should know that H.K. is my brother, P.T. is my sister.

I think I've told you more about how I write than you really want to know. I'm reminded of the famous quote of Otto von

Bismarck, which goes something like "You don't want to know how sausages and laws are made." Perhaps that applies to columns as well.

In any event, I truly enjoy having the opportunity of voicing my views in writing, and I hope you enjoy reading them.

Ed Koch on Everything

ONE

Racism Is Alive and Well

*Excerpted From Remarks
to the National Review Institute
Saturday, March 5, 1994*

In 1964, I along with thousands of other young men and women, went to Mississippi and elsewhere in the South to assist in the program initiated by black organizations to register potential black voters. The group was mostly white and preponderantly Jewish.

I spent a week in Mississippi and the only place I felt comfortable in the course of that week was in the black community, either in the church where we met to plan strategy, or in the home of black citizens where I spent each night. Everywhere else, in Jackson and in Laurel, the city where I actually tried cases and was subject to mob threats, I was very frightened—not of blacks, but of whites.

This was an historic moment for me personally and certainly for the nation. In the church every night we sang "We Shall Overcome" with great feeling.

Today, most whites, myself included, if we are alone would feel very uncomfortable in a totally black neighborhood, particularly at night, and would probably have much less fear in a white neighborhood. What has happened in the last thirty years?

Well, Jesse Jackson summed up the reasonableness of white fear in black neighborhoods, particularly at night, when he recently said, "There is nothing more painful to me at this stage in my life than to walk down the street and hear footsteps and start thinking about robbery—then look around and see somebody white and feel relieved."

So the fear is not irrational.

To provide the full story, when Jackson was later condemned for telling what clearly is the truth, he gave an explanation that is ludicrous and one which damages his integrity. He said, in effect, what I really meant was that if I saw a white face I knew that whites were moving into the neighborhood and there would therefore be more cops around. Poor man. Fear, plain fear of his colleagues had to cause him to so demean himself.

Nevertheless, he is quite special and there are moments when he exhibits extraordinary courage, as for example when Khalid Abdul Muhammad, a surrogate for Nation of Islam leader Louis Farrakhan, appeared at Kean College in New Jersey and engaged in a rant that was anti-white, anti-catholic, anti-gay and anti-semitic. In a moment I'll cite some of that language.

When, two months later, major sections of Muhammad's speech were published in a full page ad in the *New York Times* that was paid for by the Anti-Defamation League, Jackson subsequently demanded that Farrakhan denounce Muhammad. There were few if any other black leaders with the courage to do that.

But Farrakhan, rather than denouncing his surrogate's words, reemphasized them by objecting to the form not the substance. Said Farrakhan, "I stand by the truths that he spoke."

Following Farrakhan's "rebuke," Jackson copped out. Instead of denouncing Farrakhan for his failure to repudiate the substance of Muhammad's remarks, Jackson commended Farrakhan, "for taking action to discipline his national spokesperson."

Why did Jackson do it? Well, there are different kinds of fears. In the first instance, the fear was of breaking with the pack and opening himself up to criticism from other black leaders for exposing what former New York Police Commissioner Ben Ward called "our dirty little secret," referring to black crime before a black audience. Ward was booed by distinguished leaders of the New York black community who didn't want to hear his candid and truthful remarks.

There is a second kind of fear, and that is fear of death or physical assault. One explanation for Jackson's retreat was given by a distinguished columnist, Juan Gonzalez, who can accurately be described as being on the left. In his February 4th *Daily News* column, Gonzalez wrote, "According to sources close to him, he [Jackson] received several veiled threats from Farrakhan supporters who consider him a traitor for his recent comments."

Should the Nation of Islam be feared with respect to physical retaliation? Ask the widow of Malcolm X, Betty Shabazz, whose husband was assassinated by members of the Nation of Islam. According to Juan Gonzalez, at two recent New York rallies Farrakhan "brought Abdul Azziz, Aka Norman 3X Butler, who served more than twenty years in prison for assassinating Malcolm, up on stage to be publicly recognized."

Now let me talk about black crime and then I will discuss Farrakhan—who I believe cannot be blithely brushed aside and has to be taken seriously—and what we are witnessing in this country with black racial rhetoric demonizing whites, Catholics, gays, and Jews.

With respect to crime. In New York City, 57 percent of those in prison are black and 35 percent Hispanic. According to Department of Justice Statistics, 45 percent of the crimes of violence in this country are committed by black males, who are only 6 percent of the population. And black males aged fifteen to twenty-four, who are 1 percent of the population, are responsible for at least 19 percent of the murders.

It is true that large numbers of these crimes are committed black on black, but what difference does that make? If a black victim is brutalized, it makes no difference to whites if it is by another black instead of a white, or that the victim is black not white. They are still frightened by the violence as are the overwhelmingly majority of blacks who are law-abiding.

Several years ago, if I cited these violent crime figures I would have been attacked as a racist even though they are accurate. I take some credit for having been willing to cite them in a quest for truth and in order to bring attention to the cancer of crime, realizing that unless the cancer is identified you cannot treat and remove it.

It has now become acceptable to discuss black crime. In the Senate, it was Bill Bradley who two years ago had the courage to step onto the Senate floor and say, "In politics for the last twenty-five years, silence or distortion has shaped the issue of race and urban America. . . . There are two phenomena here. There is white fear, and there is the appearance of black emboldening. . . . You snatch a purse, you crash a concert, break a telephone box, and no one, white or black, says stop. You rob a store, rape a jogger, shoot a tourist, and when they catch you, *if* they catch you, you cry racism. And nobody, white or black, says stop."

And President Clinton himself last November called for an end to the violence in a speech to black ministers at the Memphis church where the Rev. Martin Luther King Jr. delivered his last sermon. Said Clinton, "I tell you, unless we do something about crime and violence and drugs that is ravaging the community, we will not be able to repair this country."

It is interesting to note that the *New York Times*, in its traditional role of denigrating jail time for criminals and always seeking to identify the "root causes" of crime, sought to link minority crime not so much to personal responsibility, as the president did, but rather to vicissitudes with which the individual could not cope, making him or her more victim than perpetrator.

Unlike Herman Goering, who said, "When I hear the word culture I reach for my gun," a repulsive Nazi thought, I must honestly say that when I hear the words root causes, I want to go to the nearest window, as Peter Finch did in *Network*, and yell, "I'm mad as hell and I'm not going to take it anymore."

I agree wholeheartedly with what British Prime Minister John Majors said concerning those two ten-year-olds in his own country who were accused of kidnapping and murdering a toddler: "I feel strongly that society needs to condemn a little more and understand a little less."

Unless we deal with the disaffiliated in our central cities, who are overwhelmingly, but not exclusively, black and Hispanic, and who often turn to crime, we will not overcome the enormous racial division in our society.

I have two suggestions on how that can be done. We should now institute a mandatory national service corps, requiring all dropouts and new high school graduates to serve for two years.

Unlike the military, it should not exclude drug addicts or those with criminal records. The key is to remove those who are disaffiliated from their existing environment.

In addition, we should institute a system whereby any person completing service in the corps who has a criminal record would be eligible for an executive pardon allowing them to start fresh. To be eligible, they would have to have gotten their GED (high school diploma equivalent), been off drugs for three years with weekly testing, and not been convicted of a crime in that period. With such a pardon, when they apply for a job and are asked, "Have you ever been arrested?" and "Have you ever been convicted of a crime?" they will honestly be able to answer, "No." It will give them an opportunity for a new start.

Of course, there are some crimes for which such pardons should not be available: murder, rape, pedophilia, to name a few.

And I also think—and the juvenile crime statistics bear it out—that earlier intervention than the corps for eighteen-year-olds is necessary. The government should fund a larger program similar to the Boy and Girl Scouts and encourage all children to join at age six or seven. It should be available every day after school to keep kids off the streets. Without structured, social interaction early on, a corps for eighteen-year-olds will be too little, too late.

Finally, let me say to those who don't want to accept the crime statistics I have cited, alleging that it is racism that causes these arrests, I would point out to them that in Washington D.C., with a black mayor, a black city council, and many black judges, 42 percent of black males aged eighteen to thirty-five in 1991 were awaiting trial, in jail, or on probation. Across the river in Baltimore, also with a black mayor, etc., it was 56 percent.

So it's not racism. Yes, racism does exist, but it cannot be blamed for the deplorable state of the black underclass in this country.

It must be noted that in the last thirty years, black mayors have been or are in charge of major cities in this country, including Chicago, Detroit, Los Angeles, New York, Philadelphia, and hundreds of other smaller cities. Currently, blacks have elected forty members to the Congress, many of whom hold high positions in the leadership, including a U.S. Senator, Carol Moseley Braun from Illinois, a state that has a black population of only 12 percent. And the highest position in our armed forces was held until recently by General Colin Powell, a black man who would be a popular candidate for President if he were to run in '96.

So it is not racism.

Pulitzer Prize-winning columnist William Raspberry wrote, "Racism hasn't gone away. But it seems obvious that racism is a less powerful barrier than it once was. Young people who earnestly desire success and are willing to work for it seldom are denied that success solely on account of race. So why is it that millions of our youngsters are not successful, and show no signs of becoming so?" And he added later, "We need a crusade to save our children as broad-based as the 1960s crusade for civil rights . . . and I freely confess, I don't know how to create it."

Now let me turn to the Farrakhan phenomenon. There are those who do not wish to deal with him and who dismiss him as unimportant. That is exactly what happened in the 1920's in Germany with respect to Hitler. I see Farrakhan as Hitler was in the 20's. I do not want to wait for the equivalent of 1932 when he took power. In a recent poll of blacks conducted for *Time* magazine, Farrakhan was the second most popular black leader with 9 percent. Number one was Jesse Jackson, who now has embraced Farrakhan, with 34 percent. In addition, in a survey conducted by a University of Chicago professor, 62 percent of the African-Americans surveyed said Louis Farrakhan represents "a positive view within the black community." It would be a serious error to dismiss Farrakhan out of hand.

What is it that makes Farrakhan acceptable to mainstream black leaders and organizations? It is their failure to deal with black crime, the drug culture, and the pathology of illegitimacy, where 66 percent of black children are born out of wedlock, and in Harlem it's more than 80 percent. These leaders are throwing up their hands and looking to Farrakhan who, with his demagogic anti-Semitism and racism, has done for blacks what Hitler did for a dispirited German population. The Führer told Germans their condition wasn't their fault, it was everybody else's fault, particularly the fault of the Jews, and that is exactly what Farrakhan is saying to blacks.

Farrakhan tells his people they are better than white people—not just equal to white people, but better than white people. And, as reported in a March 5, 1994, *New York Times* article, "According to the Nation [of Islam], whites were created by

Yakub, the mad scientist, as a test for the superior black race, who are the chosen people, and also as a curse on it."

Farrakhan's surrogate, Khalid Muhammad, also castigates whites. In November in the speech at Kean College which I mentioned earlier, Muhammad said, "We don't owe the white man nothin' in South Africa. . . . If he won't get out of town by sundown, we kill everything white that ain't right in South Africa. We will the women, we kill the children, we kill the babies. We kill the blind, we kill the crippled, we kill 'em all. We kill the faggot, we kill the lesbian, we kill them. You say why kill the babies in South Africa? Because they gonna grow up one day to oppress our babies, so we kill the babies."

Talking about Jews, Muhammad said, using an exaggerated, false Jewish accent, "The Jews have told us, the so-called Jews have told us, Ve, ve, ve suffer like you. Ve, ve , ve, ve marched with Dr. Martin Luther King, Jr. Ve, ve, ve were in Selma, Alabama. Ve, ve were in Montgomery, Alabama. Ve, ve were on the front line of the civil rights marches. Ve have always supported you. But let's look at it. The Jews, the so-called Jews, what they have actually done, brothers and sisters, is used us as cannon fodder."

Concerning the Pope, Muhammad said, "Go to the Vatican in Rome, when the old, no-good Pope, you know that cracker. Somebody need to raise that dress up and see what's really under there."

This week, after what the press called Khalid Muhammad's softer speech at Trenton State College in New Jersey, we are supposed to believe he had an epiphany. But just two weeks ago, it was clear Muhammad continued to carry his banner of bigotry. According to the *New York Times*, in a speech delivered to a black women's group in Baltimore, Muhammad "referred to Jews as 'slumlords' and 'bloodsuckers of the poor,' adding: 'It's that old no-good Jew, that old imposter Jew, that old hook-nose, bagel-eating, lox-eating Johnny-come-lately perpetrating a fraud, just crawled out of the caves and hills of Europe, so-called damn Jew.'"

Last weekend Farrakhan and his "demoted" aide appeared together at Nation of Islam Savior's Day celebrations at the University of Illinois in Chicago. According to the *Times* Farrakhan, referring to Mr. Muhammad's "bloodsuckers" remark said, " 'I didn't say it, Khalid did,' and added, 'Did he lie?' 'No,' the crowd roared back."

Is this new on the part of Farrakhan and the Nation of Islam? No. This has been going on for years. For years the Nation of Islam has been selling a libelous tape to the public which states that Jewish doctors are deliberately infecting black children with AIDS.

When Farrakhan is challenged, his defenders claim they don't subscribe to his anti-Semitic, anti-Catholic, anti-white, anti-gay rhetoric, but are simply supporting his anti-drug, anti-crime efforts to instill pride in young black males.

As a result of their turning to Farrakhan, we witnessed a shocking spectacle last September when the Congressional Black Caucus, the NAACP, and Jesse Jackson's Rainbow Coalition announced, at a panel discussion which I saw on C-Span, that they were joining in a "sacred covenant" with Farrakhan. Farrakhan was one of five panel members addressing the all-black audience, which applauded and cheered his every statement. His co-panelists were Jesse Jackson, NAACP President Ben Chavis, Rep. Kweisi Mfume [D-MD], head of the Congressional Black Caucus, and Rep. Maxine Waters [D-CA], cheerleader for the L.A. rioters.

To its credit, the *New York Times* editorially chastised Kweisi Mfume for his incredible capitulation when he announced the covenant with the Nation of Islam. But the *Times*'s denunciation was muted, more in sorrow than in anger, saying simply, "The chairman of the black caucus ought to know better. Perhaps his membership can teach him." Would they be so gentle with white leaders engaging in a pact with sowers of hate?

Perhaps some members of the black caucus can teach Mfume, as the *Times* said. But that has not yet occurred. When the House of Representatives recently overwhelmingly adopted a resolution denouncing the hate-mongering speech of Khalid Muhammad, twenty members of the black caucus voted in favor, but eleven voted against it, four, including Mfume, voted present (a recorded vote indicating an unwillingness to express an opinion) and three didn't vote at all. Can you imagine the outcry if, on a House resolution condemning David Duke, a comparable number of the thirty-two Jewish members of the House had voted "No" or simply "Present" or didn't even bother to vote?

Some extraordinary leaders in the black community, like Congressman John Lewis of Georgia, a giant in the civil rights movement, have shown enormous courage by standing up and separating themselves from some of their colleagues in the black caucus. On the House floor during the debate on the Muhammad resolution, Lewis said, "I deeply feel we have a moral obligation and a mandate and a mission to speak out against the remarks made by Khalid Abdul Muhammad at Kean College. Mr. Muhammad delivered a poisonous and a hateful speech . . . these remarks represented an obscene and ugly attack on decency . . . any time such hateful expression rears its ugly head, it should not go unchallenged."

Black leaders quite correctly say to white America, "You cannot tell us who our leaders should be." I agree, but I say to them you cannot expect decent white people, whether they be Christian or Jew, to embrace black organizations that have embraced Farrakhan and his ilk, who threaten the lives of all whites, if we are to believe his spokesman Khalid Muhammad, and engages in the vilest of slanders against Jews, Catholics and gays.

A major problem for whites is that they believe they must patronize blacks, and not hold blacks and their leaders to the same standards they would hold all others. That is racism. Many whites believe they must debase themselves if a black is not willing to discuss the issues and simply charges white racism on the part of the individual who raises the very real issue of black racism. Many blacks claim that blacks can't be racists because they have no power. Untrue on all counts. But most whites will not fight the tide and will fold, asking to be forgiven if so charged, when there is nothing to be forgiven for.

At this point we should say to black organizations that we can no longer accept their explanations that they are only supporting Farrakhan's positive anti-crime and anti-drug messages. It would be just as unacceptable if someone sought to separate David Duke's concern for the white underclass in Louisiana from his racist rhetoric. You cannot segregate the good from the bad in a demagogue.

I believe the dialogue should end, at least for now.

Finally, after the Grammy Awards Tuesday night the press made a big deal about Frank Sinatra's speech being cut off and Bono's use of a four-letter word on live television. But I saw no reference to the fact that a member of the rap group Digable Planets included Farrakhan's Nation of Islam in his litany of thanks. The crowd roared its approval without any discernible protest. Talk about a stark example of "defining deviancy down."

That show-biz crowd would have applauded Adolph Hitler if he'd worn a red ribbon.

TWO

Selected Correspondence

The Shrill *Voice* Has a Short Memory

September 14, 1993

Christopher R. Lynn, Esq.

Dear Chris:

Many thanks for your supportive letter which appeared in the *Village Voice*. Donna Minkowitz has no sense of history or what I did to support the gay and lesbian community beginning with my first Executive Order in January of 1978 ending discrimination against gays and lesbians in government. At this point in my life, I couldn't care less about what Donna Minkowitz thinks, but I do care about what you think.

It is interesting that Governor Cuomo, acclaimed for his voice of moral authority, remains governor after 12 years without accomplishing the passage of a State law which would protect New Yorkers from discrimination based on sexual orientation. New York City residents do have such protection, and I'm proud to have been primarily responsible for it.

Donna Minkowitz objects to the fact that I declined to promise rewards to Council members who would not support the then-proposed legislation and states that I rewarded members who supported tax abatement measures and should have done the same in support of gay rights legislation. It is simply not true. I never rewarded or punished Council members based on how they voted, but I did seek to persuade them to vote for controversial measures which I supported. In the drive to gain votes for the gay rights legislation, I even offered to give political support to those with whom I disagreed on other matters if they would vote for it. While some did, others did not, either out of fear of public disapproval or conscience.

I am also proud of the fact that my administration appointed to positions of authority—including commissioners and judges to the criminal, family and civil courts—New Yorkers who were publicly gay.

One final comment which you may find interesting. I was the only public official, then a congressman, to be present and supportive at the request of the gay committee seeking permission from the Parks Department to hold the Gay Rights parade in Central Park during the Lindsay administration. As Mayor, I authorized that parade to use Fifth Avenue, a privilege granted only to organizations grandfathered in during the Lindsay and Beame administrations.

Donna Minkowitz castigates me for supporting the re-election of Tom Cuite who was opposed to the legislation on grounds of conscience. I have no regrets in supporting his re-election. His help in getting other essential matters through the Council was vital.

All the best.

Sincerely,
Edward I. Koch

Setting the Record Straight

September 15, 1993

Mr. Todd Purdum
The New York Times
229 West 43rd Street
New York, New York 10036

Dear Todd:

Your article on David Dinkins is one of the most courageous articles of its kind to ever appear in the *New York Times*. Few reporters would be willing to state bluntly that the Mayor of the City of New York is not a nice person, taking into consideration the way he acts towards those whom he oversees as compared with the extremely considerate demeanor he exhibits to his peers. Furthermore, since this letter is intended to convey my criticisms, I want to repeat what I have said on a number of occasions. You are one of three New York reporters whom I have lauded as being the best in ability and fairness over all those I have known.

Over the years, I have found that unless I take exception to a reporter's statement about me which I believe to be unfair or factually incorrect, it will be duplicated by him and by others who have access to the newspaper's morgue. It is unfair of you to refer to me, as you have on several occasions, as racially divisive, or worse, engaged in the "exploitation of racial and ethnic rivalries." On a prior occasion, June 13 [there were other articles, but I haven't kept them], you said, "Mr. Koch was widely considered to have lost because he had come to be seen as racially divisive." Undoubtedly, there are some in this City, maybe many, who saw me as such, but I am concerned that your language gives it your imprimatur as true. I want to point out how unfair it would be to convey that statement as a truth.

I served as Mayor for twelve years. In my first election, I had the broad support of the black leadership, and I received 50 percent of the vote in the general election. I made a concentrated effort to eliminate the corruption which existed in the poverty programs administered by this city. Ending the use of those programs for political purposes irritated many black and white leaders who were replaced because of incompetence or corruption.

I appointed many blacks to high government positions never held by them in prior administrations, and more black judges than all the mayors before me in the aggregate, but I received little credit because they weren't recommended to me by the black political leaders or hadn't worked in the political clubs. They were selected on their individual ability, many without political references. When I appointed one particular black Deputy Mayor, I was told by a major black politician, "He doesn't count. He's yours. Not ours."

When I ran in 1981, I received 75 percent of the vote, and at that time, I was given bipartisan endorsement by both major parties, something that had never occurred in the history of this city. As I recall, I carried almost all, if not all, of the city's assembly districts. In the 1985 primary, when I ran against Herman Farrell, a black candidate, I received 38 percent of the black vote while he received 40 percent according to the exit polls. In the general election, I received 78 percent of the vote and believe I carried every assembly district in the city.

From a historical point of view, the margins of my victories were really quite astounding. I am the only Mayor to have ever attempted running for a fourth term [LaGuardia, Wagner, and I being the only three mayors in the modern era to have served for three terms]. We can debate why I lost. Some will say that it was a result of the murder of Yusuf Hawkins. I don't think so. Although, it undoubtedly added to the margin of Dinkins's victory. I believe my defeat was based primarily on longevity.

You will recall that Dinkins did, indeed, make race an issue in the 1989 campaign. I did not and neither did Rudy Giuliani in the general election. Dinkins said, "My mere election will change race relations in this City." Indeed, it did. They have been polarized to an unbelievable extent which is a great disservice to this city. Let's have lunch.

All the best.

Sincerely,
Edward I. Koch

Who's Obnoxious?

October 11, 1993

Letters Editor
Newsweek
444 Madison Avenue
New York, New York 10022

To the Editor:

I read Joe Klein's article entitled, "Dinkins's Fractured Mosaic," which appeared in the October 11 edition of *Newsweek*, and I was interested in his references to Mayor David Dinkins and me.

Joe refers to Mayor Dinkins's "fierce civility." It is interesting that he ignored the *New York Times Magazine* article of September 12 written by Todd Purdham. In referring to Mayor Dinkins, Purdham begins his article by stating that "He is not so nice." Purdham went on to say:

"There is also a Mayor Dinkins the public rarely sees, whose surliness can reduce a supporter to tears, who makes important visitors wait while he fusses over a typographical error in a speech, who eats three-course meals from china and crystal in front of aides or guests given cold turkey sandwiches on plastic trays, who does not like being contradicted but won't make decisions until he absolutely has to, who often won't tell his commissioners or the public what he really thinks and then complains that people don't understand him or do what he wants."

In describing me, Klein says, "His predecessor, Ed Koch, was a more familiar Noo Yawk type, fast, funny and obnoxious."

Isn't it interesting that Klein, who so far as I know never supported me in any one of my four elections, ignores the fact that in my second election I received 75 percent of the vote and in the third 78 percent. And even in my fourth and unsuccessful race against David Dinkins, I received 42 percent of the vote. Does he believe that Noo Yawkers are in the vast majority masochists who deliberately elect an "obnoxious" mayor? I suspect that it is an obnoxious Joe Klein foisting his personal feelings on *Newsweek* instead of engaging in an analysis of Noo Yawkers.

Now that I am a columnist writing for the *Daily News* and appearing on radio and television, all of which Joe has done or is currently doing, I would like to suggest a paraphrase to Joe of Mayor Dinkins's comment, "Don't dis your bro."

Sincerely,
Edward I. Koch

Racist "Art"

May 28, 1993

Mr. Philip H. Geier Jr.
Board of Trustees
The Whitney Museum of American Art
945 Madison Avenue
New York, New York 10021

Dear Mr. Geier:

I thought you would be interested in the enclosed letter that I received from a listener to my daily WABC call-in program. The individual was denied admission to the Whitney Museum's Biennial Exhibition for refusing to wear the admission button that read, "I can't imagine ever wanting to be white."

When your director, David Ross, heard of the complaint, he called me. He stated that the practice would be changed, but defended the exhibit alleging that there was no intent to denigrate whites. I don't know if he is right or wrong in his interpretation, but it is obvious that the Whitney Museum would never allow admission buttons to be distributed which read, "I can't imagine ever wanting to be black."

Whether or not additional corrective action is required, I leave to you. Mr. Ross said that while the regular Whitney admission buttons would not be made available during the Biennial Exhibition, a substitute such as a piece of paper would be available. I believe that his solution leaves much to be desired. I would appreciate knowing your thoughts on the matter.

All the best.

Sincerely,
Edward I. Koch

Defending My Record

November 8, 1993

Mr. Bob Herbert
The New York Times
229 West Forth-third Street
New York, New York 10036

Dear Bob:

I read your *New York Times* column, "The Verdict," and must tell you that I'm both disappointed and angry. I have always held you in high regard as a writer and as a friend and valued our conversations and occasional dinners. That was why I was shocked to read your diatribe. It would never have occurred to me that in pursuit of your agenda to soften the impact of the defeat of a black public official, in this case Mayor Dinkins, you would one day use your column to smear me by making false and irresponsible accusations.

You say, "What the city initially saw in Mr. Dinkins is what it got." Let me tell you what David Dinkins said we were getting. "My mere election [his] will change race relations in this town," was the raison d'etre he gave for running, throughout the 1989 campaign. Race relations did change; they got worse. You may not be aware of the fact, although I did tell you when you last called, that in 1989 *Newsday* found that 2 percent of New Yorkers believed race relations to be a major issue. Yet, four years later, in a recent *New York Times* poll, 67 percent said race relations were poor. Is that my fault or David Dinkins's fault? Don't you think your readers should have been told that in the context of your attack upon me? You go on to say:

> When voters went to the polls four years ago they were fed up with the cacophonous Ed Koch era—the endless confrontations, the corruption scandals, the incessant racial strife, and a sickening string of police brutality incidents. They hoped to usher in a quieter period.

"Cacophonous"? Maybe, but, "endless confrontations?" With whom? The press? With militants seeking to get their way through physical or vocal intimidation? I have no regret in standing up to the press. And I certainly have no regrets for having stood up to the militants—black, white and Hispanic— who sought to impose their wills and agendas upon this City, not at the ballot box, but through the use of intimidation.

"The corruption scandals"? I am aware of only the PVB scandal. Surely, you are not referring to the near daily corruption of civil service-appointed inspectors that occurs in every administration, which I will also discuss. The PVB scandal was not detected by any law enforcement agency in New York City—D.O.I., U.S. Attorney or district attorney—but by a U.S. Attorney in Chicago who learned of it through a phone tap.

When you say, "In one of the extreme cases ever of see-no-evil, hear-no-evil, Mr. Koch insisted that he had not been aware of any of the corrupt goings-on," are you implying that I lied and that I knew corruption existed at the PVB? Don't you think that the law enforcement agencies, trying to catch the biggest fish they could, would have sought to prosecute me if they thought I had known or had lied about it? Even when Rudy Giuliani was condemning people in my administration, he specifically said in April 1987, "I think I know as much about these investigations as anyone knows . . . including a lot of confidential material and there's not a single shred of evidence or suggestion that Mayor Koch knew of crimes that were being committed by several of the Democratic leaders and the borough presidents, or had any involvement in those crimes, or would have done anything other than turn them in if he had found out about them."

You were an investigative reporter, the bureau chief of the *Daily News* at City Hall and its Metropolitan Editor. Did you know of the corruption at PVB? Do you know of any other investigative reporters who did? Were you and your colleagues derelict as investigative reporters in not uncovering this corruption and bringing it to the attention of law enforcement authorities?

In a further reference to corruption scandals, which you describe as "spectacular and debilitating," you say that "Several top city officials and dozens of lower ranking figures were driven from office in disgrace." Let me say that I accept political responsibility for everything that happened in my twelve years as mayor. I am also ashamed of the fact that we had a PVB scandal, and I accept responsibility for that. However, it is

important to point out that the top City officials accused of corruption in the PVB scandal—Donald Manes and Stanley
Friedman—were not appointed by me. Manes was indepen-
dently elected as Borough President, and Friedman was inde-
pendently elected as Bronx County leader. Manes died by his
own hand before trial. Friedman was tried. On conviction, I
asked the court to impose the maximum sentence, and it did.

Yes, there were two lesser, but important, officials who were
also involved: Jeffrey Lindenauer and Lester Shafran.
Lindenauer was in city government before I became mayor. I
have never met him and was totally unaware of his existence
until Manes requested that Lindenauer be appointed as first
deputy at the Department of Transportation. Lindenauer's
name was submitted, along with all others, for examination on
the merits; Manes was told there were better qualified candidates and his request was denied by me. This all happened
before the PVB scandal was made public by law enforcement
agencies. Can you imagine the field day that you and other
reporters would have had had I appointed Lindenauer to a
higher post at the request of a political supporter who held not
only a vote on the Board of Estimate but was the leader of the
Queens County organization? Do you think there are many
mayors who would have denied such a request made by another government official and important supporter in the middle
of an election?

Lester Shafran was also in government before I became
mayor and had been an assistant district attorney with a fine
reputation. It turned out that he was corrupt. I doubt that even
you think I knew he was corrupt. Is it surprising that there will
be corrupt people in a city workforce of more than 250,000
people? Of the several hundred people whom I appointed to
high-level positions over a twelve-year period, six were indicted. Do you think that is a high number compared with the
number of officials in Albany or Washington, DC, who were
prosecuted during that same period?

If your reference to dozens of lower ranking figures is to inspectors in the PVB and other agencies, how do you explain that in every administration, including Dinkins's, corrupt inspectors are constantly being uncovered. They were in my administration, and in the administrations of my predecessors and, more recently, they were discovered in the Dinkins administration. I was the first mayor to place inspectors general in each agency. When you say, "There were scores of criminal convictions," in the same sentence in which you refer to Donald Manes, you are clearly seeking to convey that they were part of the PVB scandal when, in fact, they were not. Were you trying to color or hype the matter?

Let me refresh your recollection about the current PVB scandal. While those top city officials—Manes and Friedman—accused of corruption in the PVB scandal during my administration were not appointed by me, Dinkins's high-level appointees have been singled out by D.O.I. as major participants in the current PVB scandal. Those who stand accused of questionable behavior are Phil Michael, Director of the Office of Management and Budget, whom Dinkins fired, and Norman Steisel, First Deputy Mayor, whom Dinkins should fire, but refuses to. We now also know that Donna Blank, Assistant Director of the Mayor's Office of Operations, in the first instance told D.O.I. investigators that lack of recall prevented her from answering 250 questions. She subsequently, perhaps after being made aware of the fact that the "I don't remember" syndrome can be the basis of a perjury charge, came back and responded to 150 of those questions. It's been reported that many of her answers reflected adversely on the First Deputy, and neither of them has been fired. That could not have happened in my administration.

"A sickening string of police brutality incidents"? Do you remember Police Commissioner Ben Ward saying that the police officer accused in the Eleanor Bumpurs case, which you cite, performed exactly as he should have under the police regulations adopted earlier under Bob McGuire and continued under Ben Ward? Those new procedures changed earlier regulations which had provided for nets to be used to restrain EDP individuals because netting was deemed too demeaning. Ben Ward changed the regulations after the Eleanor Bumpurs tragedy. You seem to forget that a trial jury acquitted the police officer in that case. And you are holding me responsible for the death of Eleanor Bumpurs?

The Michael Stewart case, also cited by you, involved the Transit Police who are not under the authority of the mayor but the authority of the MTA, a state agency. The police actions in that case were deplored by me.

Regarding the deaths of Michael Griffith and Yusuf Hawkins during my administration, you seem to forget that those who were responsible for their murders were excoriated by me, apprehended, tried, convicted and sent to jail. In the Dinkins administration a Jew, Yankel Rosenbaum, was murdered, and his murderers have yet to be apprehended. In the August 1989 murder of Yusuf Hawkins in Bensonhurst, when one of the defendants was convicted on lesser charges in connection with the slaying, Mayor Dinkins said, "Racism allowed members of the mob that killed Yusuf Hawkins to take up arms against people they considered outsiders." Following Lemrick Nelson's acquittal, there was not one word in the mayor's initial press release about the anti-Semitism of the perpetrators, and it wasn't until after Nelson's acquittal fourteen months after Rosenbaum's murder that the mayor posted a $10,000 reward for the capture of his killers. On the Rodney King verdict, the mayor immediately said, "Found guilty or not, these four officers clearly crossed the thin blue line between appropriate response and excessive force." The mayor's outrage was not duplicated in the death of Yankel Rosenbaum.

You also mention the Central Park jogger case and the Tawana Brawley case in the context of David Dinkins being elected "to soothe the city, to help it recover from a series of extremely traumatic events." Are you suggesting that I am in any way responsible for the fact that black and Latino youths engaged in an outbreak of so-called wilding which caused enormous injury to a young woman? And is it your view that I am responsible for the fraud perpetuated by Tawana Brawley who was supported by many people, including Bill Cosby, and others leaders in the black community as well as black newspapers?

You say, "For the most part, the voters wanted Mr. Dinkins to calm things down." Did he? I don't think so. You lightly refer to "a controversial transfer of stock from Mr. Dinkins to his son [and Mr. Dinkins's difficulty in explaining it]." I'm sure you are aware that the special investigator, Elkan Abramowitz, was unable to get Mayor Dinkins's son to come in from out of state and testify under oath. Do you believe that if the mayor had asked his son to come in and give his testimony under oath to clear both of their names, he would have refused his father's request? At the end, Mr. Abramowitz said of the inquiry, "We have not cleared him. . . .We have simply concluded that the evidence is legally insufficient to warrant a criminal prosecution."

You lightly refer to the fact that the mayor failed to file income tax returns for four consecutive years. Was Comptroller Harrison Goldin mistaken when he said in the first mayoral primary debate in 1989 that no white candidate could run with a record of failing to file income tax returns for four years?

You say, "Mr. Dinkins did calm the city." You refer to the Crown Heights riot as "a tragedy" and to the Washington Heights rioting as "disorders." You laud the Mayor by referring to Los Angeles "and several other cities [which] erupted violently after the Rodney King verdict and New York did not." Are you aware of the fact that there were assaults on whites in Harlem that night and looting on lower Sixth Avenue? Are you aware that in other cities with white mayors there were no such incidents, e.g. Chicago and Boston? Isn't it racism on your part to assume that because blacks riot in Los Angeles they will riot everywhere else in the country unless there is a black mayor?

It is interesting to note that the day following the publication of your column in the *Times*, Anna Quindlen, a critic of my administration on various issues over the years, said in referring to me in her column:

> During his first term, through force of personality and his restoration of a down-on-its luck bankrupt town to something of its former fiscal glory, Ed Koch gave the illusion that like it was was possible. But he could only do so because he assembled an able staff of deputy mayors and commissioners to make municipal government what it needed to be. Just as it is commonplace to meet a respected legislator who seems dumb as a post and then be told, 'He has great staff,' so much of the confidence in City Hall comes, without voters even knowing it, from first-rate deputy mayors and commissioners. The mayor gives the municipal monster a face. But those people make it move.

In reference to Mayor Dinkins she said:

> Mayor Dinkins did not have that. Many of his commissioners were latecomers, or lackluster, and his communication with them came filtered through a haze of middle men. "I'm having a hard time getting to see him," I told one near the beginning of the administration. "So am I," the commissioner replied ruefully.

While I have always believed that you were a journalist who did not see life through race-colored glasses, I was wrong. It is truly more in sorrow than in anger that I have taken the time to write this extended letter.

All the best.

Sincerely,
Edward I. Koch

My Mind Is a Terrible Thing to Lambaste

October 14, 1993

Mr. Christopher Ruddy
The New York Guardian
316 Great Neck Road
Great Neck, New York 11021

Dear Chris:

Your interview of me is splendid, but there are some errors. You state, "Remember after one of his newsworthy strokes, a brain doctor remarked that Ed Koch may have the body of a sixty-plus-year-old male, but he still had the brain of a thir-teen-year-old." Firstly, I had only one stroke. Secondly, the doctor announced at a well-attended press conference that my brain, having been measured against 15,000 other brains, was that of a twenty-eight-year-old. I am not flattered that you referred to it as the brain of a thirteen-year-old.

About two years ago, when I had an attack of atrial fibrilla-tion, I had a pacemaker inserted, and another doctor held a press conference. This time the doctor announced that at sixty-six, I had the body of a forty-two-year-old. Now, I'm going to tell you something that has not been the subject of a press con-ference. When I recently had my PSA and prostate examina-tion, another doctor told me that I had the prostate of a twenty-five-year-old. I am now trying to bring brain and body into closer alignment.

As the prime detector of the errors in the PBS film *Liberators*, you were responsible for their ultimately withdrawing that film and correcting the record. I would hope that you would feel compelled to do the same here.

All the best.

Sincerely,
Edward I. Koch

The *Times'* Radio Daze

The following is my letter to the *New York Times* responding to their editorial. I spoke with Howell Raines, the *Times*'s editorial page editor, who told me that, "We are not printing your letter because it is too ad hominum in its attacks. You don't know where the members of our editorial board live and whether they live in areas that have prostitution. If you want to take those sections out, we will print it." I said, "No, I'll put the whole letter in my next book," as I did on an earlier occasion years ago with a letter that they wouldn't print unless I excised a paragraph. Here it is:

February 25, 1994

Letters to the Editor
The New York Times
229 West Forty-third Street
New York, New York 10036

To the Editor:

The *New York Times* in its editorial ["Radio Free Patronage," February 23, 1994] attacks Rudy Giuliani for exercising his right as mayor to suggest to the president of WNYC that he consider hiring Curtis Sliwa. That same *New York Times* editorial attacks me for having required WNYC when I was mayor to broadcast the names of convicted johns on the radio in order to deter prostitution which was destroying neighborhoods. I still believe that such a "john hour" would deter prostitution, and it is used in other jurisdictions. In fact, I would recommend to Mayor Giuliani that he reinstate the "john hour."

What is particularly galling about the *New York Times* editorial and position is that for years the *Times* published the names of restaurants that had not been convicted but merely cited for alleged health code violations. I guess the difference is that the *New York Times* editorial board has an interest in clean restaurants. After all, the board's members don't live in the neighborhoods that prostitution is destroying.

New York Times editors are not concerned with prostitution. Why should they be? They are not even concerned about heinous crimes. The editorial board is filled with people who believe that there are already too many people in jail; that we should stop building prisons; that we should end the death penalty; that we should stop arresting low-level drug dealers (as if high-level drug dealers sell on the street and destroy neighborhoods); that we should use alternatives to jail by putting bracelets on criminals' ankles allowing them to remain at home rather than to be incarcerated.

The police estimate that 1,500,000 felonies occur every year, of which one million go unreported because citizens have concluded that government doesn't care. The *Times* is most concerned with what they refer to as "root causes." Sure, let's attack the root causes, but until we're successful, let's put people in jail who commit crimes, particularly crimes of violence.

The mayor of the city is comparable to the publisher of the *New York Times* vis-a-vis WNYC. Publishers tend at the *Times* to be benign in the exercise of their authority, as mayors are with WNYC. Nevertheless, the publisher of the *New York Times* has at times exercised that authority. For example, when the editorial board intended to endorse Bella Abzug for the Senate over Pat Moynihan, the publisher directed that the *Times* endorse Moynihan, and it did. He was absolutely right to do so. The current publisher surely by order, winks, nods and shrugs influences current editorial policy. It is his right. And it is the right of Mayor Giuliani if he wants to exercise his authority—and I don't know if he did—to direct WNYC to hire Curtis Sliwa. Does it make it more acceptable that a city appointee, Tom Morgan, make the hiring decisions?

The editorial board of the *New York Times* has lost touch with this city. Regrettably, they are not concerned with the pain and suffering of the vast majority of people who live here.

All the best.

Sincerely,
Edward I. Koch

THREE

Nobody Asked Me, But . . . Ed Koch on Politics

Abortion

Roe vs. Wade is alive and well. But you wouldn't know it from listening to some of the eulogies given by the leaders of the pro-choice groups.

Following Monday's Supreme Court decision, Patricia Ireland, president of NOW, said, "Roe is dead, despite the flimsy stay of execution today from the court." Kate Michelman, president of the National Abortion Rights Action League, said, "What the court did today is devastating for women." And Planned Parenthood is running ads implying that the right to use birth control may soon be restricted. How outrageous.

The current law, even incorporating the changes resulting from the court's most recent ruling, still makes the United States one of the most liberal countries in the world with respect to the right of abortion. The Pennsylvania limitations permitted by the U.S. Supreme Court—a twenty-four-hour waiting period, informed individual consent with a discussion of alternatives, and parental consent for minors (with a judicial bypass provided)—are, I suspect, endorsed for the most part by a majority of Americans, both "pro-choice" and "pro-life." A New York Times/CBS poll conducted shortly before the decision showed that the majority of Americans favor having some limits set by the states.

So why are pro-choice leaders denouncing the court, predicting back-alley abortions and generally sounding the tocsin? For political purposes, to expand their membership and increase fund-raising. While many thought this decision would push the abortion issue out of the political arena, I suspect there will be an effort to escalate the rhetoric for the dual purpose of defeating George Bush and the laudable goal of electing more women to Congress.

These goals shouldn't be achieved by inflaming the public, falsely stating the end of the right of abortion and creating panic. Nor should pro-lifers be twisting the truth as they have been. While there are certainly some partisans on both sides acting solely out of conscience, there are many who are fanning the flames in order to retain their power on the political scene.

The most outspoken and zealous opponent of all abortions, and the most florid and vile, Randall Terry of Wichita fame, said: "Three Reagan-Bush appointees stabbed the pro-life movement in the back." Terry should appreciate the exercise of one's conscience.

His reference to Justices Sandra Day O'Connor, Anthony Kennedy and David Souter should have caused the pro-choice spokespersons to applaud those same justices. Foolishly or by design, the attorney for the pro-choice complainants threw down a gauntlet before the court, arguing that any change in the original Roe vs. Wade decision would be a rejection of the right of women to have an abortion. The three justices could have said, "OK, if that's what you want, we'll give it to you."

Fortunately, O'Connor, Souter and Kennedy—all of whom had been selected because the president who nominated them believed they would strike down the right of abortion when given the opportunity—didn't pick up the challenge. Had Clarence Thomas joined them in their majority opinion, he would have vanquished his detractors, who are legion. But instead, he performed to expectations. The real surprise was Kennedy appointee Byron White.

Issues like abortion, the death penalty and euthanasia are matters of conscience, and those whose opinion is not the current law will continue to seek to change the law. That is their right, indeed their moral obligation. The abortion question will be raised every time a president nominates a new Supreme Court justice. But, as we have seen, the person selected doesn't always perform as a president expects. That, too, is the marvel and strength of our democracy.

In my book, the Supreme Court as a whole deserves praise for having exercised independent judgment in construing the law consonant with their conscience and oath of office. And those of us who support choice should be shouting hosannas in praise of O'Connor, Souter and Kennedy.

(7/3/92)

Abstinence

Remember the editorials in the daily papers (the *Post* excepted), encouraging schools to tell kids to use condoms and mocking the teaching of sexual abstinence in New York City public schools? Condoms were viewed as almost panaceas, abstinence an impossible dream.

An Oct. 4 editorial in the *New York Times* is a minimalist apology. It points out, "School programs that teach abstinence can delay the onset of sexual activity and, once activity begins, reduce the frequency of intercourse and the number of sexual partners." The editorial cites an Atlanta program in which the students are trained "to develop the social skills to resist sex . . . By the end of the eighth grade . . . only 8 percent of the boys who participated had begun having sex, compared with 29 percent of those not in the program . . . Only 1 percent [of the girls] had started having sex, compared with 15 percent." So, abstinence is not necessarily a hopeless cause as some have said.

(10/16/92)

Actors Equity As Censor

When is censorship not censorship? When it is being exercised by Actors Equity.

The union has gone on record to denounce as censorship any restrictions on National Endowment for the Arts grants. So what should we call its own demand that producer Cameron McIntosh (*Cats, Phantom of the Opera*) hire only an Asian actor for the lead part in the Broadway debut of *Miss Saigon*? The role in question is that of a Eurasian pimp—part Vietnamese and part French. It is currently being performed in London by Jonathan Pryce, who is a recognized "star" under Equity rules and is entitled under comity with British Equity to play that particular role in the United States. But because Pryce is Caucasian, American Equity says he shouldn't be allowed to perform here.

What hypocrisy. During the height of the controversy surrounding the restriction of NEA grants that would support the public display of obscene artwork, such as that by Robert Mapplethorpe, Actors Equity ardently denounced as censorship any proposals to limit government funding on the basis of content. It is hard to believe the union doesn't see the rank hypocrisy of its position. But after all, don't these matters depend on whose ox is being gored?

I saw the musical *Miss Saigon* in London. It is truly an extraordinary theatrical performance. Jonathan Pryce is brilliant in the lead. By rights he should play it on Broadway. But American-Asian actors, like B.D. Wong, the star of the Broadway hit *M. Butterfly*, object to Pryce being cast in the role because it would be a lost opportunity for a young Asian actor. Actors Equity agrees with Wong when he says Asian actors "may never be able to do the real work we dream to do if a Caucasian actor with taped eyelids hops on the Concorde."

Isn't there something ludicrously wrong with Wong's logic? If theatrical roles are to be assigned on the basis of race, ethnicity or religion, what happens to art and the true performer? Does it mean that because she is black, the great Jessye Norman should be denied the role of Sieglinde in Wagner's "Die Walkure," which she does so extraordinarily well? Should the wonderful singer Hei-Kyung Hong be denied the role of Gilda in "Rigoletto"?

If Wong were to follow his reason to its logical conclusion, he would be hoist with his own petard because, by his own way of thinking, the role in "M. Butterfly" should have been played by a transvestite. Colleen Dewhurst, president of Actors Equity, recently said in opposition to Jonathan Pryce being allowed to play in New York: "Everybody should be in an uproar because whoever does this role will become a star." Does B.D. Wong sleep uneasily having prevented some budding transvestite from attaining star status? Moreover, isn't it just as racist to say that only an Asian can play the role of the Eurasian pimp in *Miss Saigon*, when the character is as much European as Asian?

Acting and the theater involve magic, theatricality, illusion and grace, all of which call upon the skilled actor to exhibit facets and personalities totally foreign to his or her race, ethnicity, training and background. That's what makes it art.

In the case of *Miss Saigon*, the proponents of racial casting are denying a bona fide star the right to play the role he created. Is that fair? Is that art? Isn't it racism to think otherwise? Apparently not for Colleen Dewhurst and Actors Equity.

In a radio advertisement denouncing restrictions on National Endowment for the Arts grants, Colleen Dewhurst said: "Imagine a world in which millions of people are at the mercy of a small band of extremists, in which works of art are subject to government censorship, and freedom of expression is a crime. Now stop imagining, welcome to America 1990." Replace the words "government censorship" with the words "union censorship," and Ms. Dewhurst could just as well have been describing the restrictions she, along with B.D. Wong and others, want to impose on the American theater. Under current conditions, *Miss Saigon* should stay in London until the weather changes.

(8/3/90)

AIDS

This past Sunday, the *New York Times* published posthumously an in-depth article on AIDS written by Jeffrey Schmalz, a *Times* reporter who died from that disease in early November. The *Times* had allowed Schmalz to report regularly on AIDS, an unusual assignment because he had become an advocate for a cause.

In this case, the *Times* was right to have allowed it. Schmalz gave us insights into the feelings of those who suffer from this terrible disease because it was he who was suffering. His writing brought out the human devastation caused by this modern plague.

Schmalz wrote, "The treatments simply are not there. They are not even in the pipeline . . . I am getting sicker. Time is running out . . . Once AIDS was a hot topic . . . Now, twelve years after it was first recognized as a new disease, AIDS has become normalized, part of the landscape. The world is moving on, uncaring, frustrated and bored."

Frustrated? Yes. Uncaring and bored? No. Unlike Schmalz, I don't believe interest in AIDS has waned. The advocates have been zealous in keeping the issue up front. The country has not lost interest—but it is repressing the horror that it feels.

In the course of their life time, one out of nine women will get breast cancer. 60 percent of the autopsies of all adult males show they had localized prostate cancer at the time of death. Many more Americans will die from various forms of cancer than from AIDS. Yet more money is spent on AIDS research as a whole, and more concern is given to it. Why? Because of the special terror it arouses, and because the majority of those dying from AIDS are in the prime of life.

Schmalz points out in his article that most experts believe no cure for AIDS is in sight, since there is currently no cure for any virus-caused disease. There are vaccines to prevent a handful of viral diseases—for example, polio and hepatitis—but an AIDS vaccine is not expected until after the year 2000.

If we accept the obvious, there is only one course of action and that is to take those initiatives that are within our control to reduce AIDS infection. The causes of most cancers have not been identified and cancer cannot be prevented, although changes in diet, habits and environment can have a significant impact. But AIDS can be.

It's especially important in light of the fact that young homosexual males, who were in grade school when the disease first surfaced, are not taking the risk as seriously as they should. In his article, "Tempting the Virus," journalist Charles Kaiser wrote, "Much of this activity is among those men too young to have experienced AIDS up close; for them the notion that a single night of unprotected intercourse can eventually cause one of the most hideous deaths imaginable remains completely unreal."

It would be foolish to suggest that adults give up sexual activity. It would be equally foolish to believe vast numbers of heroin addicts can go cold turkey and immediately stop shooting drugs. But lifestyle changes, using condoms while having sex and clean needles when shooting drugs, can greatly reduce the chance of getting AIDS for homosexuals and drug addicts, who comprise 80 percent of those afflicted.

To that end, I wrote in July of this year to a hundred people in Hollywood: actors, directors, studio heads and theater owners among them. Instead of just wearing red ribbons, making contributions to AIDS organizations and hosting fund-raisers, I suggested to these "movers and shakers" that they use their influence to help create acceptable, short films educating the public on the use of condoms. To that, we should add the need for clean needles.

These films could then be shown in movie theaters around the country during the intermission between showings.

Only a half dozen bothered to respond and convey their support. The most interesting response came from a director who wrote, "Part of me goes, 'What a great idea!' Another part of me goes, 'Yikes!' Condom ads would have them racing for the exit or at least embarrass everybody so much that it could get the feature presentation off to an uncomfortable, awkward start!' "

I appreciated that director's honesty. But he knows that the short films need be no more explicit than the movie's rating warrants. If it's sensibilities against saving lives, is there any choice?

(12/3/93)

Woody Allen

Right into the middle of this explosive political campaign focusing on family values drops Woody Allen, America's most famous neurotic.

I've spoken with Woody Allen twice. The first time was when I did a cameo in the movie *New York Stories*. I played myself, New York City's mayor, holding a press conference at Gracie Mansion. Since Allen never lets the actors know what the full plot is, all I knew was that I was defending the right of a mother to fly around Manhattan like a bird, giving advice. I did it to his satisfaction in only three or four takes, which I'm told is remarkable. That wasn't my first movie role. I had been in *The Muppets Take Manhattan*.

About a year later, I saw Woody Allen at Elaine's. I went over to him and said in my most humble, supplicant voice, "Mr. Allen, do you remember me? I was in one of your movies. Did I end up on the cutting-room floor?" He said, "No, you were rather good, and you are in the movie." I left on a high note.

Now this screwed-up brilliant bundle of neuroses, who has been in therapy for most of his life, is in deep doo doo. Technically, he has not committed incest. But morally he certainly has. He has forgotten there is a line between guardian and ward. In Dickens's *Bleak House*, the guardian acted as a guardian should. Woody should read it.

Unfortunately, his id took over. It's not surprising that a young woman like Soon-Yi became infatuated with her quasi-stepfather, especially with one so worldly and a celebrity, who had been part of the household since she was a child.

Soon-Yi attacked her mother this week, saying, "I was not raped, molested or manipulated as Mia has hysterically charged . . . To think that Woody was in any way a father or stepfather to me is laughable. We rarely ever spoke, and were polite but uninterested in one another." And, "I don't think Mia should go on adopting children. I don't think you can raise eleven children with sufficient love and care." She seems to have chosen to forget that she was one of those adoptions.

That Allen could become infatuated with this young woman is understandable. But it wasn't because they didn't talk or have eye contact, but rather because they did. But fundamental decency—I'm talking about the recognition of a universally accepted taboo—required that he not allow the affair to commence. If the primordial urges were so extraordinary, he should have taken a cold shower and prevailed on Mia Farrow to send Soon-Yi on an extended trip abroad and allowed maturity to produce its own results. He failed the test.

I give scant credence to the allegation that Allen sexually molested his adopted seven-year-old daughter or, as was originally alleged, also his four-year-old son. It is so heinous an accusation that it should not be believed by the public unless and until sufficient credible evidence is produced to substantiate it.

Some Republican attack dogs despicably see this tragic situation as manna from heaven. Over the weekend, Newt Gingrich said, "I call this the Woody Allen plank. It's a weird situation, and it fits the Democratic Party platform perfectly." The Bush/Baker team has apparently decided not to rein in political bully boys like Pat Buchanan and Gingrich. It's not enough for the president to say they don't speak for him. He has an obligation to denounce them.

There are some who see this vileness as evidence that the Republicans, in their fear of losing the election, will do anything to retain office. I once thought, and said, that it was unfair for President Bush's critics to denounce him for saying, "I'll do anything to win." I didn't think he would violate common decency. I no longer feel that charitable, based on what occurred at last week's convention and the way the Republican campaign is shaping up.

Woody should have taken the advice of his mother flying over Manhattan, who no doubt would have whispered, "Incest is not for us, sonny."

(8/28/92)

James Baker

My disclosure in this column a few weeks ago of Secretary of State James Baker's disparaging remark concerning Jewish voters ("F___ 'em. They didn't vote for us") caused quite a stir.

One of the most hostile reactions came from Al Hunt, Washington bureau chief for the *Wall Street Journal*. In a television appearance, Hunt charged that the column "smacks of a politically inspired smear." My letter to him follows, shortened for space purposes:

"Your ad hominem attack on me requires that I first give my credentials. As I am sure you know, I served five terms in Congress, receiving 78 percent of the vote in my fifth election. I am one of three mayors in the modern era, LaGuardia and Wagner being the other two, to have served for three terms and, even though I was defeated, I am the only mayor to have run for a fourth term. Mayor Dinkins received 50 percent of the vote, and I received 42 percent.

"Now to the substance of your attack. My column of March 6 had the following reference to Secretary Baker: 'In fact, when Baker was criticized recently at a meeting of high-level White House advisers for his belligerent attitude toward Israel, he responded, "F___'em. They [the Jews] didn't vote for us." Baker uses every opportunity to denounce Israel's right to allow Jews to live on the West Bank. According to Sen. Patrick Leahy, in addition to blocking the loan guarantees, Baker wants to cut Israel's existing foreign aid as a penalty for constructing settlements on the West Bank.'

"In your comments on CNN, you referred to that column as an outrage of the week. You also said the following: 'The *New York Post* front-page banner headline charges Secretary of State Jim Baker has made obscenely derogatory remarks. Who's the source? *Post* columnist Ed Koch, the former mayor rejected by the voters two years ago. Eddie Koch is even less credible as a journalist than as a politician. That story smacks of a politically inspired smear.'"

Two *New York Times* columnists have verified that the incident occurred. In fact, William Safire's comments were far more pejorative than mine. On March 19, he reported the following: "At a Bush speech the other night, a White House aide sought me out to say, 'You know, Baker never said that.' "

Safire's column continued: "Though constrained by the rules of deep background, I can confirm that Mr. Baker did say that, with the same vulgarism that made it so memorable, to two high officials on two different occasions. President Bush and his top staff know he did; it has been agreed that everybody would deny it was ever said. But James Baker said it—twice—and meant it. (Years from now, memoirs will confirm this; I'll remind you.)"

Leslie Gelb reported the following in his March 19 *Times* column: "I don't doubt Mr. Baker said it, despite his denials."

My question to you is, having attacked me, will you now alert your listeners, watchers and readers to the fact that two distinguished columnists have verified what I reported? If not, why not?

Let me give an additional observation. I believe that the number of terms a public official is allowed to serve should be limited. I think it would be good for the country to have new officials elected on a regular basis to break up the symbiotic relationship that they have formed with members of the press.

As a result of your reportorial comments, I have come to the conclusion that a similar rule should apply to reporters, especially Beltway correspondents. People like you, who love the fact that they cover and work with the highest officials in the land, such as Secretary Baker or Henry Kissinger or the president himself, become co-opted with the passage of time. Because of their desire to continue their exclusive and intimate contract not given to lesser reporters, these reporters protect those people they are supposed to cover.

Let me ask you a professional question: Don't you think it served some journalistic purpose to learn of Secretary Baker's remark? Had you learned of it from an impeccable source, as I did, would you have published it? If not, do you believe that Safire and Gelb violated a journalistic rule? If not, is there a different rule that applies to me?

(4/3/92)

Book Reviewers

This column could be called "Advertisements for Myself."

This column is my reaction to a *New York Times* review of my new book, *Citizen Koch*. For some reason the *Times* assigned this review to its television critic, Walter Goodman, a man apparently more at ease evaluating television's "Twin Peaks" than reviewing books, and apparently obsessed with sex.

Mr. Goodman is distressed that in the book, which covers, as he writes, "growing up Jewish in America: immigrant parents, Depression years, encounters with anti-Semitism, the Catskills, service in World War II, New York's City College . . . the one striking omission is sex . . ." For Goodman, this is "all the more striking" considering Dan Paisner's previous coauthor was Geraldo Rivera. Dear readers, you may recall that when Geraldo, whom I respect as a talk-show host and reporter, wrote his autobiography, he mentioned every lady he ever bedded. One of them, Bette Midler, reacted by saying: "He was a bad lay." Nevertheless, Goodman apparently was titillated.

I deliberately chose not to discuss my sex life. I referred in my book, as Goodman does in his review, to "the subject of [my] unwedded state and the rumors of homosexuality . . . Whether I am straight or gay or bisexual is nobody's business but mine." But Goodman disagrees: "The rules are different in a book that purports to be the story of a life." He apparently believes that writing an autobiography constitutes a waiver of every aspect of one's personal privacy.

Goodman's interest is not in information, but in the pursuit of prurience. And he is no longer an adolescent. He notes: "There is not a word here about . . . [his] first visit to a whorehouse." Let me make a confession. I never went to a whorehouse. Did he? And who cares?

Am I offended by his review? Not really. Reviews sell books. Am I surprised? Indeed I am. Why would an erudite television critic be so hung up on sex? Does he live his sex life vicariously? When he reads Winston Churchill's books, does he look for chapters on his sexual activities? If Margaret Thatcher pens her autobiography, will he be disappointed if she fails to disclose her sexual escapades other than perhaps mentioning her husband?

Goodman may feel cheated that in 281 pages—which I hope most people will find a good read, taking them through sixty years of my life—he did not find a second Geraldo. But remember, Mr. Goodman, my sixth, seventh and eighth books are yet to be written. And who knows what evil lurks in the hearts of men?

(9/18/92)

Bosnia

Who killed Cock Robin? All his "friends" in Western Europe who take every opportunity to express their devotion to freedom but refuse to give the Bosnian Muslims arms to defend themselves.

Who'll sing a psalm? "Not I," says German Chancellor Helmut Kohl, who began the destruction of Yugoslavia by rushing to recognize Croatia and Slovenia as independent states against all advice.

Who saw him die? "Not I," says John Major, Britain's weak-kneed successor to Margaret Thatcher. When she called for bombing attacks, a member of Major's cabinet reacted by saying the Iron Lady was too emotional.

Who caught his blood? "Not I," says France's Socialist president, François Mitterrand. When he thought it would help his party in the recent elections, he made a dramatic flight to Sarajevo to show his solidarity with the Muslims. Has he made a return trip?

Who'll make the shroud? "Not I," says Secretary of State Christopher. He went to Europe to get support for military action against the Serbs, but it was a charade with a wink and a nod on his part.

Who'll dig his grave? "Not I," says Lord Owen. But that's exactly what he has done. He told the world, "Lifting the embargo would, in my judgment, fuel the intensity of the war," thus depriving the Muslims of arms to defend themselves.

Owen now recommends that the Bosnian Muslims accept a Serb-Croat plan that would chop Bosnia into three parts and allow Serbia and Croatia to absorb large sections of territory, Shades of Neville Chamberlain.

Who'll be chief mourner? Presumably Cyrus Vance, former partner in the Owen-Vance peace plan, who told *New York Times* columnist Anthony Lewis that when he thinks of Bosnia he is "sad."

Who'll carry the coffin? Every one of the members of NATO, including Turkey, and the twenty-two Muslim Arab states that are standing aside while their co-religionists are slaughtered. It is so easy for these Arab states to declare a jihad against the small state of Israel, yet these same nations refuse to send soldiers or arms to help the beleaguered Bosnian Muslims.

Who'll toll the bell? President Clinton. When it comes to culprits, perhaps he is the major one because he could have made the difference. During the campaign, he criticized President George Bush for failing to lift a finger to help the Bosnian Muslims. But when he took office, he reneged on his promise to provide the Muslims with arms.

Now he deceptively says, "If the parties themselves agree, genuinely and honestly agree," the U.S. would have to look closely at the Serb-Croat plan. Again, shades of Neville Chamberlain.

The world is witnessing a repetition of what the democracies failed to do during the Spanish Civil War. Franco's Fascists received arms from Hitler and Mussolini. Loyalist Spain received nothing from the West. I would not send one American soldier to any part of the former Yugoslavia: that is for the European nations of which Yugoslavia is a part. But it is a moral imperative for the U.S. to provide arms to defenseless Bosnia and let them decide whether they want Munich or Masada.

Air Force Chief of Staff Gen. Merrill McPeak has said that the Air Force could safely bomb and eliminate the Serb artillery currently destroying the so-called safe havens set up by the

United Nations for Muslim civilians. Isn't what McPeak is suggesting far less dangerous to American military personnel than Clinton's agreement to provide as many as 35,000 ground troops as "peacekeepers"? Those American soldiers would be sitting ducks in the guerrilla war to come. Just look at Somalia.

Who killed Bosnia? Will President Clinton have the candor of the sparrow and admit, "It was I, with my inaction and duplicity, that let Bosnia die"?

(6/25/93)

Carol Moseley Braun

Carol Moseley Braun, a freshman senator, recently engaged in the courageous act of berating her colleagues. Enraged that the Senate had approved extending a patent for the Daughters of the Confederacy to use a version of the Confederate flag, Sen. Moseley Braun demanded that the Senate repudiate its vote. Her arguments were direct, emotional and, from her point of view, rational. But the Senate, in rescinding its decision, was direct, emotional and irrational.

During the Senate debate, Sen. Moseley Braun said, "Why would we give an extraordinary honor to the symbol which is counter to the symbol that we as Americans, I believe, all know and love, which would be a recognition of the losing side of the war. . . ."

Why? Because Americans know that every region in our country is proud of its unique characteristics. Yes, Southern charm, hospitality, patriotism and courage are well known throughout the land.

Today, Southern support for the Confederate flag has no connection with the concept of slavery. Everywhere in this country we have come a long way on race relations. The best example is Illinois—where support for the Confederacy was strong in the southern part of the state—which elected the first African-American female senator in the person of Carol Moseley Braun last fall. As Sen. Moseley Braun said, "I am here today. My state has less than 12 percent African-Americans in it . . ."

That change, the acceptance of people on the basis of their credentials and character rather than the color of their skin, is at least as prevalent in today's South as it is in many places in the North.

Seeking to deprive the South of its history by having the Senate denigrate a symbol won't bring us together.

This issue has come up in different form before. In 1975, when I was a member of Congress, we voted to restore the citizenship of Robert E. Lee. The House vote was 407 to 10. Two of those opposed were Bella Abzug and Elizabeth Holtzman. Apparently, they were ahead of their time.

(8/6/93)

George Bush

President Bush is reportedly in a state of deep depression over his loss to Bill Clinton. Let me reassure him, and I say this from personal experience, the best is yet to be.

In May 1991, I had a meeting with President Bush. I asked whether the dog sitting nearby, who looked nearly comatose, was best-selling author Millie, and the vice president told me she was. When I arrived back at my office I told everyone, "That dog is sick." Later on, it was reported that Millie, like the president and Mrs. Bush, was suffering from Graves' disease, a thyroid condition. So, you see, I have some medical qualifications, having detected the symptoms before the veterinarian did.

As we entered the Oval Office, the president said to me, "What are you doing with yourself now, Ed?"

I said, "I am a partner in the law firm of Robinson Silverman, and I also speak around the country under the auspices of the Harry Walker Agency."

He asked, "Is he still getting 30 percent?" I replied, "Yes," recalling that before he became president, George Bush had been a horse in that same stable. "And," I added, "Harry is worth it." The president said, "I'll bet you can't wait to run for office again."

I said, "Mr. President, you are so wrong about that. I am enjoying my new life and will never run for elective office again."

The president then said something that shocked me. It was: "I can't wait to get out of here."

Startled, I responded, "Mr. President, don't say that. You have six more years to go," since at that point he was in the middle of his first term. Little did I know that I was privy to Dr. Freud speaking through the mouth of President Bush.

I mention this because, upon reflection, it is now clear the president did not have his heart in the 1992 campaign. Many people, myself included, who observed his lackluster responses and lack of energy thought perhaps it was related to his health.

I discussed the matter with my own physician, Bruce Barron. His thesis, based simply on what had been reported in the press, was that in treating the president for Graves' disease, the doctors had to walk a fine line in determining the appropriate amount of medication to provide him with the energy he needed, without aggravating his atrial arrythmia heart condition. He speculated that the president's advisers feared an arrythmia episode that could cause him to pass out temporarily, a devastating blow to a re-election campaign. He couldn't afford another debacle like the one that occurred in Japan.

Harry Walker will undoubtedly be calling President Bush, and I'm sure our paths will cross on the lecture circuit. I hope so. I also believe that the president's great talents, particularly his international expertise, should be utilized by his successor. The phrase "The king is dead, long live the king" applies even to a kingless nation. But wouldn't it be a stroke of brilliance for the new king to break with tradition? In that event, I hope President Bush accepts the challenge.

(11/20/92)

Caning

This column was written for the German publication, Frankfurter Allgemeine, *May 1994.*

Michael Fay has been caned, survived and probably will never commit another crime, at least in Singapore.

If caning were reintroduced in the United States—and that would require a constitutional amendment since it was outlawed as unconstitutional by the Supreme Court in 1948—I believe crime would be vastly reduced.

The government of Singapore is not a Western style democracy, nor is it a dictatorship. It is a government, unlike the U.S., that gives much greater weight to the needs of broad society than to the individual.

On balance, I prefer our democratic government, and I'm sure that those living in Germany, especially those who experienced the totalitarian government of Adolph Hitler, would likewise prefer to continue under a Western democratic regime. Nevertheless, within Western-style democracies, there can be room for change—and caning.

If one were to compare the rates of criminality in the U.S. and Singapore, one would have to conclude that living in an American city is infinitely more dangerous than living in Singapore. Based on 1991 figures, the number of murders per 100,000 in the U.S. is five times higher than in Singapore. Robbery and motor vehicle theft are also five times higher. Burglary is ten times higher and forcible rape thirty-two times higher.

I propose that we restore caning, or, as we say in the U.S., flogging, but American style: not quite so heavy handed as apparently is the case in Singapore. Fortunately, bamboo doesn't grow in the U.S. So we would use a leather strap, very much like the strap my father used on me as a juvenile and to good effect. It left no open cuts, there was no bleeding, but the pain, in actuality and memory, remained with me for a long time.

I like to think it helped formulate my character in a positive way. When I complained to my father about it, saying "Papa, it hurts," he responded traditionally, "It hurts me more than it hurts you." I think he really meant it, even though I didn't accept it at the time.

There are those, like Amnesty International, who describe flogging as torture. Torture like many things is—to some extent—in the eye of the beholder, not necessarily determined by the seat of the recipient. What I mean is that there has to be a consensus worldwide on what is and is not torture at a given time in history. One man's torture is another man's passing pain.

A definition of torture that is sometimes used describes it as the infliction of intense pain to afford sadistic pleasure. Caning does not meet that definition. Society is not engaging in sadism. It is merely defending itself. Similarly, the death penalty cannot be defined as torture, it being used in thirty-six states in the U.S. and in many countries that are members of the UN.

I support the death penalty. And, so long as it is acceptable to major sectors of our society worldwide, those sectors in opposition do not have the moral or legal authority to outlaw it worldwide. Some will say, "Does that mean horrendous genocidal acts by a particular nation, such as the former Nazi Germany, or existing Arab Nations that apply a religious law which allows the severing of limbs as appropriate punishment for certain crimes, cannot be described as unacceptable?" The answer is no. The consensus I refer to must include not only the nations within which the punishment is permissible, but an acceptance of what is being done by large numbers of people in countries where the practice is forbidden.

Let me again illustrate. Germany, France and England do not have the death penalty, and citizens of those countries who oppose capital punishment can provide a whole host of reasons for their opposition to those who believe it should be restored in those countries. Yet I am convinced there are many Germans, French and English who feel there are crimes for which it would be appropriate to restore the guillotine or its equivalent, such as premeditated murder or the murder of a police officer.

So it cannot be said there is a universal consensus opposing the death penalty. But there surely is consensus opposing genocide in any nation, and the severance of limbs everywhere outside of Arab countries. There is no consensus opposing caning. Indeed, even in England and the U.S. today, and probably in Germany, corporal punishment is not prohibited except for prisoners. So, while corporal punishment cannot be inflicted on those committing the worst of crimes in the U.S., it may be inflicted on students. How bizarre.

I continually ask the following question whenever I speak before any audience: "If you believed that flogging convicted drug dealers would reduce recidivism, perhaps eliminate it, would you support it?" Ninety percent or more generally say yes. To the few hands raised in opposition, I simply say, "Oh, you've invited a few social workers." And the audience applauds wildly.

In the U.S. we have allowed the rights of society to be denigrated by relatively small numbers of criminal predators who are making our lives miserable. I believe that we should try flogging in addition to prison and see if it doesn't vastly reduce or eliminate crime, both quality of life offenses and the more violent, vicious crimes. If, after a reasonable time, it hasn't worked, we can go back to what we have now: lawlessness on the part of many who know they will not be punished at all under existing laws.

Jimmy Carter

At the Democratic Convention Jimmy Carter, emulating the style of Mario Cuomo, said, "There are two Atlantas . . ." He described one as a "wonderful city, prosperous, progressive and blessed with good racial relations." But, he said, in the other

Atlanta, "neighbors . . . rotated the boiling of water from street sewers." I find that hard to believe, but if it's true, it happened under Governors Carter, Busbee, Harris and Zell Miller and under Mayors Massell, Andy Young and Maynard Jackson. Why does Carter see the Atlanta on "the shining hill" as the product of local Democrats, and the other Atlanta as the fault of Ronald Reagan and George Bush? Hypocrisy.

(8/7/92)

Fidel Castro

It is amazing that some radicals in this country still support Castro's Cuba despite the fact that he continues to oppress his people with his communist agenda. Now Americas Watch and Amnesty International have reported that the Castro government is organizing local vigilante groups to terrorize dissidents. In November, poet Maria Elena Cruz Valera was beaten, dragged by her hair from her home and placed under arrest. Dozens of others have been similarly detained by groups of civilian volunteers. Castro's actions mirror Daniel Ortega's, whose "turbas" (vigilantes) terrorized Nicaragua's citizens before Ortega was deposed. What will it take to get the radical left to acknowledge that Castro is a major violator of human rights? Why aren't gay-rights organizations protesting the fact that Castro places homosexuals and those with the HIV virus in detention camps?

Censorship

The *New York Times* has declared that the National Endowment for the Arts is above criticism, and that if you criticize it you are engaging in hysteria. I disagree. I support the NEA, but that does not mean it's perfect.

In an editorial of May 17, the *Times* effectively declared that the NEA is beyond criticism because of its "shining example of . . . twenty-five years of accomplishment." The NEA has a lot it should be proud of. But it's wrong to pretend it doesn't make errors in judgment or that its procedures for awarding grants are not occasionally flawed. Its mistakes should not go unnoticed—or uncorrected.

Today's most controversial obscenity cases involve Robert Mapplethorpe and Andres Serrano, both photographers. Mapplethorpe's photos are obscene by any reasonable standard, national or local. They include photos of Mr. Mapplethorpe shoving a bullwhip up his rectum, one man urinating into the mouth of another, and other photographs similar in nature.

The other artist, Serrano, has a number of superb photos, but one is clearly so offensive that the vast majority of Americans will be offended by it. It is a crucifix placed in a tank of the artist's own urine. For me and for most people, this has to be considered sick. Like Mapplethorpe's work, Serrano's exhibit has appeared as a result of government funding through an NEA grant. Even if it's not technically obscene, should the government use taxpayer funds to display it? I think not. If artists decide to produce offensive works such as Serrano's and Mapplethorpe's, they should do so at private expense.

I believe government should provide subsidies to artists through the National Endowment for the Arts. But I also believe there has to be a better way to appeal NEA decisions, including ample notice to the public. It should be left to artist peer groups to judge proposals and award grants, but the public has a right to know what goes on in that process.

Remember the patrons of old, the popes, the doges of Venice, the Medicis of Florence, who in many cases told the artists what they wanted them to paint and sculpt? Today we don't tolerate—and we should not tolerate—the government telling artists what to paint or sculpt or write. We leave that to the artist. But nevertheless, government's decisions to fund certain works of art have to be somewhat restrictive. After all, a democratic government is obligated to seek some consensus as to what the people want their tax dollars used for.

There's a natural tension between government and the arts—and that's how it should be. The arts are irritating, and that, again, is how it should be. But why should the artist feel the government should subsidize his excesses. Do your thing courageously, but leave the government out of it. After all, Dostoyevsky never sat in his flat waiting for a check from the czar.

(6/1/90)

Bill Clinton

For me it's no longer a tough call: Bill Clinton and Al Gore deserve to win the general election. I supported Al Gore four years ago, but I am newly arrived in my support of Bill Clinton.

Clinton has survived everything from attacks on his marriage to the way he chose to oppose the war in Vietnam. Through it all, he has demonstrated enormous inner strength. Most important for me, he has also resisted the efforts of the left wing of the Democratic Party to put its stamp on the party platform, thus thwarting the left's attempts to impose its ideology on mainstream Democrats who reject its views. Clinton's courage gives the Democrats their best chance in two decades to win the presidency.

In 1981, following Jimmy Carter's defeat by Ronald Reagan, Democratic Party leaders held a conference in Baltimore to try to understand why the election was lost. As mayor of New York City, I was among those asked to speak. Here's some of what I had to say: "I believe that over the past decade, the national Democratic Party lost the sense of where it came from, what its purpose should be and what the reality facing America was all about.

"What happened over the last decade is that we became the party of the status quo, the party of government for government's sake, the party of abstraction. Rather than seeing ourselves as the inheritors of a dynamic, pragmatic, humane tradition, we sought to embalm our past successes—the New Deal, the Fair Deal, the New Frontier, the Great Society—in regulations and programs. We lost touch with reality.

"We became unable and unwilling to recast programs that, however well-intentioned, had faults. When some pointed to abuse of welfare, Medicaid and food stamps, we avoided the issue. When job-training programs did not work, we put more money in. Poverty programs provided jobs for the people running the programs, but often did not help the poor. We looked the other way. When it came to crime, though we talked tough, we consistently sided with the need to protect the civil liberties of the criminal, not the victim.

"In short, I believe we can recapture the American public by recapturing the center of American politics. I believe our strength today lies, as it did in the past, in our ability to be the party of balance, of tolerance, of competence and of common sense."

While I delivered this speech in October 1981, it would have been just as relevant at last week's Democratic Convention. Regrettably, up until Bill Clinton's nomination, the Democratic Party hadn't changed its direction.

Now it has changed. Throughout the campaign, Clinton has stood up to the special interests, not rejecting their legitimate concerns, but not letting them set the agenda. Rescuing the party from the ideology of Ted Kennedy and Jesse Jackson, he has brought it back to the principles of Hubert Humphrey and Scoop Jackson.

Clinton did not flinch from discussing controversial matters: welfare reform, his support of the death penalty, adequate defense funding, black racial bigotry as well as white. Bill Clinton didn't scare easily. He stayed the course.

Of course, there are issues and beliefs on which Clinton and I disagree. However, when I was running for office I said, "If you agree with me on nine out of twelve major issues, you should vote for me. If you agree with me on twelve out of twelve, you should see a psychiatrist." I agree with Clinton on nine out of twelve issues.

Two Democratic paladins, Clinton and Gore, rode into Madison Square Garden and brought the party back to where it should be. They took the city and the nation by storm. No doubt there will be reverses over the next several months. There always are. Those who believe in the Democratic Party as it once was—and is again under this new leadership—must be prepared for the inevitable Republican onslaught. This time the Democrats did it right.

(7/24/92)

The Coliseum Project

Since the contract for developing the Coliseum site was entered into during my administration, reporters have been calling to ask my view on the current negotiations. I'm responding here because I prefer to have my full thoughts, rather than an edited version, published.

There's a lot of money riding on the Coliseum project. The mayor ought to stop all negotiations and let things sit for a year or two as the real-estate market continues to rebound. Meanwhile, the $33.8 million letter of credit representing Mort Zuckerman's prospective penalty if he does not close the transaction under its original terms should be cashed.

It has been suggested that new appraisals be obtained for the property. Forgetaboutit. When the city received appraisals prior to the request for proposals in February 1985, they ranged from $225 million to $250 million. The highest bid was $477 million, and the accepted Zuckerman bid was $455 million. The sales price was later lowered to $338 million when the pro-

posed building was reduced in height. The only way to estab-
lish current market value is through the bidding process. To
renegotiate the contract and sell half the site for $80 million,
while freeing Zuckerman of the $33.8 million penalty, as he
proposes, is absurd.

Everyone talks about privatization in this town. So let's look
at how the private sector would deal with this issue. Assume
that either Larry Silverstein, a major developer, or Larry Tisch,
a mega entrepreneur, had owned the Coliseum site eight years
ago and entered into a contract for its sale with Mort
Zuckerman, another major developer and a friend of mine—I
hope he will remain one—and Zuckerman told Silverstein or
Tisch eight years later, "Real-estate values have fallen. I want
you to reduce the price and allow me to buy only half the site."
What would either one have told Zuckerman to do? That's
exactly what the mayor should tell Zuckerman to do.

Indeed, it's inconceivable that Zuckerman would have even
broached the issue. If he believes the law is on his side, and
insists on buying half the site at the reduced amount, let him
litigate—after the city collects on the $33.8 million letter of
credit. Even if the city loses in court, and I don't think it will, at
least New Yorkers will know everything possible was done to
protect them.

Zuckerman collected approximately $100 million from
Salomon Brothers when the latter reneged on its commitment
to become the site's prime tenant. Even after expenses, he's
already a winner—even if he has to pay the $33 million he
owes. How many tricks can one property turn?

(5/6/94)

Crime

A little passion on the part of the populace can go a long way.
This November, voters in New York State have the opportunity

to let their elected officials in the state legislature know what matters to them.

If we could construct a 20th century, idealized version of Plato's Republic, what is it that we would ask for our legislature? First and foremost, personal safety. Our assemblymen and state senators know what has to be done. But after decades of running for office with no real challengers and a passive electorate failing to hold them responsible at the polls, many of them do not see the protection of society as their top priority.

Indicative of public anger at the failure of our current criminal-justice system is the huge support among Americans for Singapore's policy of caning, which it uses to deal with quality-of-life crimes—and apparently with great success.

In the United States, we permitted flogging until 1948, when it was ruled unconstitutional as "cruel and unusual" punishment by the Supreme Court. I would not be adverse to restoring flogging as a punishment, but that can be done only by a constitutional amendment. If you knew that by restoring flogging, you could have a cleaner, safer city, would you think it was worth it? I would.

The possibilities are endless. Flogging could be used to punish those who commit criminal acts and who would otherwise never be punished at all. Also, are there many among us who would oppose flogging, in addition to prison, for spouse batterers, child abusers and pedophiles? Too often, these people are inadequately punished.

Apart from corporal punishment, what are some of the key criminal-justice issues that our legislators should be addressing?

• Welfare fingerprinting: New York and New Jersey have agreed to share computer records. It's not enough. Never underestimate the cunning of a felon: People who collect welfare in both states are smart enough to use different names, and only fingerprinting will detect them.

• Drugs: Re-evaluate current drug laws with a view toward reducing inappropriate mandatory sentences for low-level offenders, and increasing sentences for more serious drug crimes.

• Juvenile justice: All teenagers arrested for felonies should be fingerprinted and photographed. Their arrest records should be available to the Criminal Court if they later commit crimes as adults. This is not currently the case. It's enough for justice to be blind, but must it be deaf and dumb too?

• Prisons: Build whatever jail space is required to imprison every sentenced felon and violent misdemeanant.

• Parole: End it. Criminals should be required to serve their full sentences, with a reduction only for good behavior, as they are in the federal system.

• Death penalty: The death penalty will not solve the problem of crime, but it is more than merely symbolic. There are some people who commit murder that so subvert society that they deserve nothing less than a death sentence. I believe, as does the Supreme Court, that some people will be deterred by it.

In New York, we need to do for criminal-justice issues what was done so successfully in New Jersey concerning taxes. In New Jersey, a few concerned citizens got together and formed a state-wide, anti-tax committee. That organization ultimately resulted in the defeat of many of the then-majority Democrats in the state legislature, and the subsequent defeat of the incumbent Democratic governor, Jim Florio.

I actually believed that Florio's tax policy was the correct course of action and that he, and the legislators who supported him, should have been re-elected. But the ability of that citizens group to arouse the public was astonishing.

Democrats and Republicans who are moderate in their views, and are tired of the irresponsibility of those in the legislature on the radical left and the radical right, should join forces on issues where there is a commonality of interest, and form a bi-partisan election committee.

This committee should target Democratic and Republican legislators who, if they are not willing to support changes in the criminal-justice system that are designed to protect society, would be opposed by the committee for re-election in November. Money would be raised throughout the state to provide funds to the adversaries of these legislators in both the primary and the general elections.

Somewhere out there is a non-partisan, concerned citizen willing to give the time, intelligence and financial resources to lead such a committee. Step up and do your duty.

(4/8/94)

Crime and Homelessness

On the evening of Aug. 28, I decided to go to a movie with a friend in Greenwich Village. The film, called *Pump Up the Volume*, was playing at the Angelika Theater at Houston and Mercer Streets.

Since the show was to start at 8:10 P.M., we arrived at the theater at about eight and waited in line outside. People were very friendly to me. They were overwhelmingly young, single and married middle-class residents of the Village and SoHo.

I stood there conversing with the young couple in front of me; they said that they were going to leave the city since it wasn't safe for them or their children. I said, "Don't do that. Wherever you go you will not be happy. There is just no place like New York."

Then I heard someone yell my name. About fifteen feet away was someone who belonged to a group we used to describe as derelicts or vagrants, almost all of whom are drug addicts, alcoholics, mentally unstable or a combination thereof. He called out, "Eddie is here? The mayor? Where is he? Where's the mayor? I want to kiss him."

As he advanced toward me, I became anxious. His body movements and facial expressions were clearly menacing. As he closed in, Bill, my private security guard, stepped between us, arms folded. The vagrant looked at him and asked, "Are you the mayor's bodyguard?" Bill replied, "Yes." The vagrant said, "You want me to disappear, right?" And Bill said, "Yes." The person then began walking away, but said, "I'll be back, and I'll kill you."

What if I had not been accompanied by a security guard? If I had fought the derelict, who knows what might have happened, particularly if he drew a weapon? Would I have called for help or run away? How do you do that without feeling terribly embarrassed? And even if I did, what good would it do? There was no cop in sight. Would those in line come to my aid? Who knows?

It seems that these days everybody has a similar tale to tell. Another such incident took place the same week involving one of my former press secretaries. His infant daughter wanted apple juice at three A.M. There was none in the refrigerator, so her doting father decided to go to the all-night neighborhood grocery. As my friend was buying the apple juice, a vagrant saw him accidentally drop money on the floor. As my friend was leaving, the vagrant called to another one waiting outside, "He has twenty-five dollars on him." My friend didn't know whether to simply cross to the other side of the street or run. The decision was made for him as one of the vagrants began to run toward him. My friend is no athlete, but when his adrenaline started to pump he became a two-legged Native Dancer in the run for his life.

He got to his door two steps ahead of his pursuers, found it locked until the doorman opened it, and slammed it behind him. A close call.

My friend and his wife have always lived in this city. They are emotionally tied to it, as well as by family relations and by virtue of their jobs. They will never leave for the suburbs, but now they worry about their daughter's schooling and safety.

I know these incidents happen to many other people. I'm lucky I have a security guard. My friend has a doorman. But most New Yorkers—whether they live in a slum or a middle-class neighborhood—have neither. Are they at the point of giving up? Personal safety for their family, particularly their children, dominates their thoughts.

Why are we allowing this to happen to us?

(9/7/90)

Crown Heights

What did he know and when did he know it? This week's superb 600-page report on the Crown Heights pogrom recalls that crucial question of the congressional expose of Watergate. Why? Because it reveals Mayor Dinkins's loss of memory and lack of credibility.

Following the tragic, accidental death of Gavin Cato on Monday evening, August 19, 1991, the Crown Heights riots erupted, resulting in the murder of Yankel Rosenbaum. The violence was described by the report's author, Richard Girgenti, Governor Cuomo's director of criminal justice, as the most extensive racial unrest in New York in twenty years. It continued for four days.

Why did the mayor fail to intervene and prevent the pogrom, which included assaults on eighty Jews and the vandalizing of scores of Jewish-owned properties? The report states that top City Hall officials knew as early as Tuesday morning that the riot was not under control. The mayor received a phone call from his friend and adviser Howard Rubenstein on Tuesday or early Wednesday morning imploring him to intervene. His own Community Assistance Unit staff, which was in Crown Heights, reported to Deputy Mayor Bill Lynch and others that the police "gave up their positions and ran."

Additional information was available to the mayor from the five or more police bodyguards who are with him at all times. As mayor, I received such information from them, which they regularly got from the City Hall police desk, and it's unlikely the practice was changed. As the report pointed out, the City

Hall police desk logs provided the mayor with detailed information, including the fact that Tuesday evening, stores were burned and looted and that the police had been "forced out" of the area. Inspector Jules Martin, commander of City Hall, told Girgenti that all "big-ticket items" would be reported to the mayor, and Crown Heights was definitely a "big-ticketed item."

Imagine, as reported by the *New York Times*, two-hundred police officers ordered to retreat by their commander, breaking ranks, with some running from a mob instead of standing firm.

Perhaps they feared they would not receive crucial support from Dinkins and Police Commissioner Lee Brown when later on the black mob and black leaders began their inevitable chant of police brutality, as so often happens.

Despite the evidence laid out in the report, the mayor insists, "Prior to Wednesday evening I received no special allegations that the police were providing inadequate police protection or that the police were deliberately restraining their response."

His memory is worse than Ronald Reagan's.

As one perplexed reporter at the mayor's Tuesday press conference asked, "Didn't you turn on the television?" referring to the violence that was being depicted. Were the mayor's sets turned off for forty-eight hours?

The mayor is attempting to lay it all off on the police brass, who, all agree, did a terrible job led by an incompetent police commissioner. But he can't. He must assume personal responsibility for his own dereliction of duty—waiting three days to do what was required.

How many people were assaulted between Tuesday morning, when the mayor had to know the police were not doing their job, until Wednesday after midnight, when he finally exercised his mayoral authority? In that intervening forty-eight hours, the mayor was either paralyzed or indifferent.

There is no doubt in my mind we are witnessing a coverup here involving the mayor's convenient memory, as well as the memory lapses of his closest advisers, Deputy Mayor Bill Lynch and others. The report questions those memory losses at the top levels, citing two very courageous field staffers, Robert Brennan and Joseph Gonzalez, who told the investigators that they had reported to Lynch, Community Assistance Unit Director Michael Kharfen and mayoral liaison Herbert Block regarding the out-of-control riot and police failures.

The report says, "We found no reason to believe their [the field officers'] statements were less than truthful."

Last week, presumably trying to cushion the report's impact, Governor Cuomo referred to Mayor Dinkins as "an authentic American hero."

Perhaps the governor knows something we don't. But we now know that in Crown Heights the mayor failed the even simpler test of leadership.

(7/23/93)

Alfonse D'Amato

The *New York Times* editorial page occasionally lapses into double standards, and the latest occurred following Sen. Al D'Amato's reelection. Instead of congratulating the senator, notwithstanding its endorsement of his opponent, the *Times* vilified him as "a man of shabby accomplishment and indifferent ethics."

Compare that with this past Tuesday, when the *Times* attacked Bob Dole, the Senate Republican leader, for saying, "Fifty-seven percent of Americans voted against Bill Clinton, and I intend to represent that majority on the floor of the U.S. Senate." The *Times* characterized his statement as "rancorous" and "obstructionist." Shouldn't its editorial on D'Amato be similarly described? You bet.

Death Penalty

Last week, House Democrats tried to end the use of the death penalty in the United States. Desperate to secure support for the crime bill from at least some members of the Congressional Black Caucus and other liberals, they attached Racial Justice Act amendment to that legislation.

The amendment would allow those sentenced to death to use statistical evidence of alleged racial bias tainting past executions to set aside their own death sentence. A minority defendant would not be required to prove that a jury had specifically engaged in racism in ordering his death—simply citing the statistical pattern of alleged racial bias would be enough.

Rep. Don Edwards (D-Calif.) recently said in an interview: "Forty percent of the 3,000 people on death row are black, even though blacks are only 13 percent of the population." Surely Edwards, longtime chairman of the Judiciary Subcommittee on Civil and Constitutional Rights, knows, but fails to mention, that 55 percent of the murders committed in 1992 were by black perpetrators. Further, black males ages 15 to 24, who are 1 percent of the population, committed at least 18 percent of those murders. For courts to be considered non-racist using Rep. Edwards' tortured logic, 55 percent of those executed should have been black.

Using similar torturted logic, a case could be made that it is white murderers who are the subjects of discrimination. Far fewer blacks than whites have been executed: Of the 227 people executed between 1977 and January 1994, according to the NAACP Legal Defense Fund, 124 were white, 88 black, 14 Latino and one Native American. Fifty-five percent of those executed have been white, when 55 percent of those committing the murders were black, at least in 1992, the last year for which Justice Department figures are available.

The Edwards' doctrine, bizarrely, would require that juries sentence even more black defendants to death to achieve true racial balance. Isn't it fair to ask, if the number of black murderers being executed had been raised consistent with their murderous deeds, would those supporting the amendment have cheered this achievement of racial equality?

Jurors are charged by the court to limit their discretionary application of the death penalty to rational criteria established by the state, and must consider all mitigating factors helpful to the defendant. It's impossible to know why a jury condemns a particular defendent to death. The Supreme Court has said, "Jurors cannot be called . . . to testify to the motives and influences that led to their verdict."

This amendment is an attempt by the House to overturn the 1987 Supreme Court decision in McClesky vs. Kemp. In that case, the court ruled by a 5-to-4 vote that statistical evidence covering all murder sentences in a jurisdiction could not support a charge of discrimination in a particular case. Specific racial bias must be proved in each individual case.

How could it be otherwise, since the jury in each case consists of different groups of people, and, under current law, no prospective juror may be challanged on the basis of race?

As mayor, I attended the heartbreaking funerals of police officers killed in the line of duty. From 1977—when the death penalty was resumed in the United States following the Supreme Court ruling that it was constitutional—to 1994, 54 NYPD cops were killed in the line of duty. Of the murderers apprehended, seven were white, 31 were black and 13 were Hispanic.

None of those killers was executed because New York state does not have the death penalty. In its editorial supporting the "racial justice" amendment, The New York Times says, "The state might successfully rebut such evidence (of racial bias), say in a case involving a slain policeman, by showing a consistent pattern of seeking the death penalty for cop-killers regardless of race."

In view of the Times's fervid opposition to the death penalty, for them to use that example is chutzpah.

The long and the short of it is that the supporters of the racial-bias amendment are overwhelmingly against the death penalty for anyone. They know, however, that the country—and their constituents—overwhelmingly support the death penalty, and, therefore, they prefer to obfuscate when offering their support of the amendment.

When pressed, they offer the disingenuous argument that those who murder black or Hispanic victims are not put to death in the same proportion as those who murder white victims. Again, I ask: Would they be satisfied if more murderers of blacks were executed, knowing that blacks are murdered overwhelmingly by other blacks?

For the opponents of the death penalty, it's any argument, no matter how flimsy. This particular ruse is so transparent, one can only hope the Senate rejects the amendment in the joint conference.

(4/29/94)

*   *   *

It's clear that the death penalty will be one of the major issues driving this year's race for governor. The death-penalty debate will never end. Nor will the debate on abortion. Both sides on both issues believe they occupy the high ground.

As someone who supports both the death penalty and the right to abortion, I find it bizarre that many of those who oppose the death penalty on the grounds that it is uncivilized for the state to take a precious life are in the vanguard of those supporting the use of surgical abortion to end the life of a fetus.

Since 1976, when the death penalty was resumed in the United States, only 240 convicted felons who murdered other human beings have actually been executed. Since 1973, when abortion became a constitutionally protected right under Roe vs. Wade, more than 30 million fetuses have been destroyed in the womb. If there are pangs of conscience, for whom should they be?

There are four major issues usually debated when discussing the death penalty. The first being: Is the death penalty cruel and unusual punishment—and therefore unconstitutional? The U.S. Supreme Court disposed of that issue in two major cases.

The court suspended the death penalty in 1972 and said it could not be used in an arbitrary or capricious way. In 1976, when the court permitted the penalty to be resumed, it did so under specific guidelines that are accepted by the 36 states that allow capital punishment. Murder alone does not subject someone to the death penalty. Both aggravating and mitigating circumstances must also be taken into account.

The second argument is: Does the state have the right to engage in an act of revenge, retaliation or retribution? Yes, Virginia, it does. How else can one explain punitive damages awarded in civil cases? How else can one support jail time in cases that could be concluded with only a monetary fine? How else can one defend the penalty of solitary confinement? The state, but not the individual, has the right to protect itself by avenging assaults committed against society, and to show its abhorrence and anger. The synonyms for punishment may sound harsh to the ear, but they aptly describe it: Punish is the verb, retribution is the noun.

The third argument used is that the death penalty is not a deterrent. Yet, how else can one explain the decline in kidnapping following the enactment of the federal Lindbergh law. That law called for the death penalty if the victim died while being held hostage. Kidnapping is exceedingly rare today, and, in this instance at least, most experts credit the Lindbergh law and its death-penalty statute.

Professor Ernest van den Haag, in the best law-review article I've read on the death penalty, said: "Most abolitionists acknowledge that they would continue to favor abolition even if the death penalty were shown to deter." He's right—and everything else they say is verbiage. I believe there are some crimes that are so heinous and egregious that no lesser punishment than the death penalty is adequate.

While it is true that studies on deterrence are inconclusive, I would argue that the death penalty has not been utilized sufficiently and, therefore, its efficiency has not been tested. The 157 prisoners who were executed between 1977 and 1991 represent only 3.8 percent of the 4,101 who were under a death sentence during that time.

It is interesting to note that many opponents of the death penalty also oppose building more prisons. They say sending someone to prison instead of providing an alternative punishment only makes for more embittered and proficient criminals. Some of those same critics claim many criminals prefer prison to their ordinary lives, because they have better food and shelter there.

Those critics who oppose both the death penalty and prison continue to sing that tired old refrain, "Look for the root cause." In the meanwhile, society is being subjected to daily mayhem. As Professor van den Haag aptly put it, "Abolitionists appear to value the life of a convicted murderer or, at least, his non-execution, more highly than they value the lives of the innocent victims who might be spared by deterring prospective murderers."

Finally, there is the emotional issue of innocent individuals possibly being executed. To the best of my knowledge, no person has ever been executed in the United States who was later found to be innocent by a broad consensus of law-enforcement officials and others knowledgeable in the field. Indeed, those desperately seeking examples to make their case often cite Sacco and Vanzetti, as well as Julius and Ethel Rosenberg. Surely, there is no braod consensus of innocence in either of those cases.

Even if there exists the remote danger of an innocent death, I'm still for the availability of the death penalty, because society has the right to protect itself. In war, innocent civilians are always killed accidentally—they're called collateral deaths—yet *just wars* must be fought to protect nations and, with 24,000 murders in 1992 alone, the United States is involved in a losing war against criminals.

Further, there are many more cases of murderers given "life imprisonment" and getting out to kill again than there are miscarriages of justice. Who can forget the case of Arthur

Shawcross, the Rochester man who confessed to strangling an 8-year-old girl and also admitted killing a 10-year-old boy whom he later said he cannibalized? After serving 15 years of a 25 year sentence, Shawcross was released on parole and went on to kill 11 women before he was rearrested.

I've always been intrigued with how one serves two life sentences.

(5/27/94)

Dieting

I have made a major decision. It doesn't involve a $27 billion budget and 300,000 employees, but simply my desire to liberate the thin person who lives within me. I have gone on a liquid diet. It requires discipline. I have a malted drink in the morning and again at lunch. For dinner I have a meal of not more than 600 calories.

Last Saturday, I went with friends to see a Broadway show; afterward, we went to a terrific Italian restaurant in Chelsea. I ordered within my diet requirements—a small arugula and endive salad with a dressing of mustard, vinegar and garlic. No oil. Then I had an entree of broiled mushrooms with lots of garlic and a minimum of olive oil. Later I weighed myself; the weight was coming off.

The next day I went to Worcester, Massachusetts, for a speaking engagement. Foolishly, I did not take my liquid-diet ingredients with me, expecting to have a small salad at the home of my host. But this was not to be. There was no salad, only some small, heavily oiled tomatoes. And a salmon mousse.

I looked at the mousse and the mousse looked at me. There was no stopping us: I failed the self-discipline test. From now on, I'll bring my malteds with me because you can't count on a small arugula and endive salad in every American city.

After a reception, I went to the Worcester synagogue to speak to an audience of 600 to 700 people. There I saw U.S.

Rep. Joe Early, an old friend with whom I served in Congress. Joe is about five-foot-four and has always been heavy, even though in his youth he was a great basketball star.

When I saw him I said, "Joe, you look thinner." He replied, "Ed, I have told everyone here that you are an honest man and only tell the truth. I weigh 250 pounds so please don't tell me that I look thinner."

So much for the noble lie. I wasn't very good at it while I was mayor—I told the truth even when people didn't want to hear it. I think I'll stick with that policy in private life, too.

David Dinkins

The sense of fulfillment and pride evidenced in Mayor Dinkins's State of the City speech on Monday is not as pervasive in the rest of the city as it is at City Hall.

Dinkins's stated belief that his mere election would repair race relations in this town helped get him elected. Governor Cuomo believed him. You may recall the governor, after first endorsing "the old jalopy," got out of that car, crossed the street and endorsed the man "who would bring us together."

So what hath the mayor wrought over the last three years? In his annual year-end interview with the media, the mayor modestly said, "I am satisfied by my behavior."

Does the city share that view? Have race relations improved? In a recent *Newsday* poll, 17 percent of respondents singled out race relations as the most important problem facing the city, compared to just 2 percent of respondents in July 1989.

Since his perceived sensitivity to race relations was viewed as the mayor's major strength, how can this be? There are some who believe that the mayor has proved himself, that attacking him in this area is unfair, and further, will assist in his re-election.

Richard C. Wade, the unreconstructed McGovernite who teaches at CUNY, told the *New York Times*: "All the Hasidim have done is solidified the blacks and not won over any of the whites who voted for Dinkins the last time. For those people, it looks like the mayor is being put upon."

I don't know whom Professor Wade talks to. Last month's *Newsday* poll showed that many New Yorkers, not just the Hasidim, throughout the five boroughs disapproved of how the mayor handled the Crown Heights riot. That disapproval ranged from a low of 40 percent, in the Bronx, to a high of 67 percent, on Staten Island.

Questions remain as to why the mayor failed to stop the rioting immediately, instead of waiting three days—until after a bottle was thrown at him when he visited Crown Heights. Some New Yorkers—and I'm one of them—take exception to his announcing that he was "incensed" that the Crown Heights riot was being described as a "pogrom." We Jews know what a pogrom is. It's what blacks know as a lynching.

Many New Yorkers—white and black—continue to be distressed by Dinkins's comment on the acquittal of Lemrick Nelson in the murder of Yankel Rosenbaum. Dinkins said, "The criminal-justice system has operated fairly and openly in reaching this conclusion."

There are those who remember that the mayor refused to participate in a ceremony at Ellis Island celebrating that historic landmark through which millions of immigrants, including my own mother and father, poured. The mayor said, "I don't want any part of that. Ellis Island is for the people who came over on the ships! My people came over in chains." That's bringing us together?

Some recall that he allowed then-Police Commissioner Lee Brown to decline to enforce for eight months a court order restraining the picketing of a Korean grocer in Brooklyn by a black group, led by Sonny Carson. The boycotters ultimately forced the store owner out of business.

What people sense is the vast difference between the mayor's response to the Korean shopkeeper and to the Jewish community in Crown Heights compared with what his likely reaction would have been if a black merchant had been illegally picketed by whites or Bed-Stuy stormed by a white lynch mob.

When these issues are brought up, those raising them are accused by the Mayor's defenders, including some editorial writers and columnists, of playing the "race card." In fact, it is the mayor, by portraying himself as a victim, who plays the "race card" more skillfully than his critics.

At the heart of the distress, many New Yorkers feel, is Dinkins's failure to apply the same standards to all groups and, even worse, his failure to apply the law uniformly. That's what divides and angers people. Mayor Dinkins has applied the double standard again and again, and should be held accountable for it.

(1/8/93)

Drugs

Two much-admired federal judges, Jack Weinstein and Whitman Knapp, have announced they will no longer try drug cases. What flows from this movement by them—and an estimated fifty more federal judges—is an effort ultimately to federally decriminalize or legalize drugs.

Isn't that what the British did to the Chinese, when they sought to narcotize that country?

These judges say the emphasis on law enforcement over education and treatment has failed. Another federal judge, Robert Sweet, flatly states that he favors legalization: "The present policy of trying to prohibit drugs through the use of criminal law is a mistake. It's a policy that is not working. It is not cutting down drug use. The best way to do this is through education and treatment."

Wrong.

A study by the Research Triangle Institute found that even under *ideal* treatment conditions, 53 percent of cocaine addicts

the congressional contest between Joe Addabbo and Simeon Golar. Addabbo defeated Golar, who is black, in a district with a black majority. The voters recognized that Addabbo was more qualified. Similarly, Hugh Carey defeated Howard Samuels in the 1974 Democratic primary for governor, with a majority of Jews voting for the Catholic, Carey. And the percentage of votes I received from Jews in my mayoral elections was lower than the percentage I received from the Irish and the Italians.

But there is a disturbing change currently taking place in the political appeals being made by candidates. Not long ago, Mayor Dinkins went to the Convent Avenue Baptist Church, where he made a thinly veiled pitch for black votes to an assemblage of black ministers: "I need you to help me. Were it not for the black church, our people would not have survived, and if we survived slavery, we can survive anything. I know that with your continued assistance I will achieve success again. . . . I know how important you are."

Can you imagine what the reaction would be if Rudy Giuliani went to a Catholic church to make such a blatant political appeal to a group of priests? Or if I, in the 1989 campaign, had made similar remarks to a roomful of rabbis? In either case, a great cry would have gone up accusing us of breaching the sacred wall separating church and state.

It stands to reason that someone who is black, Catholic, Jewish or Hispanic should expect to get a larger share of the constituency from which he or she comes. There's nothing wrong with racial pride. But when one candidate has been clearly more qualified, New York voters have generally looked beyond shared background and chosen the best candidate. That's what voters in last year's Senate race did: Jews, in unexpectedly large numbers, voted for Al D'Amato over Bob Abrams.

But things are changing. My 1989 mayoral primary race against David Dinkins, in which he received a staggering 95 percent of the black vote, was an ominous portent for the future. Were such overwhelming numbers based solely on the merits of the two candidates? I doubt it.

In this year's mayoral election, I expect David Dinkins—who is vulnerable due to his performance as mayor—will issue a call to arms on the basis of race. Or his supporters will do it for him. One such supporter, Congressman Charles Rangel, said late last year that Hasidic Jews would have "a major problem" in New York if they continued to criticize the mayor. Rangel later wrote that his statement "was intended not as a threat . . . but as the counsel of an old friend." Really?

(5/7/93)

"Freedom Fighters?"

Isn't there something bizarre about the new, improved city council passing a resolution demanding amnesty for twenty-one Puerto Rican "political prisoners," including criminals who robbed a Wells Fargo bank in Connecticut? Councilman Jose Rivera, who introduced the resolution, referred to Puerto Rico as a "colony" in subjugation. If that's true, why is there so little support for independence by Puerto Ricans in the United States and on the island itself? They could get it just by voting for it. Regarding the "freedom fighters" resolution, why would Councilman Walter McCaffrey, otherwise intelligent, say, when referring to a bank robbery, "If in the minds of those individuals it is a political act, then I think they are doing it for a political agenda"?

City Council President Andrew Stein should be ashamed of himself for seeking radical fringe votes by gratuitously announcing he would have voted for the resolution if the law allowed him to. (The council president only votes in the event of a tie.) Some of those who voted "yes" admitted this was one more stupid resolution to satisfy one more ethnic group. They wish the council would stop embarrassing itself. Don't hold your breath.

(12/4/92)

Gays in the Military

In a recent Gallup poll, 72 percent of Americans said gays can serve effectively in the military if they keep their sexual orientation private. But 53 percent are still opposed to the president changing military policy and allowing gays to serve openly in the armed forces.

The public's response could be construed as "fear of flaunting." I think it means the general public believes that sexual orientation should not be a bar to service, but that one's sexual conduct can be subject to criticism. Members of the armed forces—heterosexual or homosexual—should not engage in sexual activity, including importuning during working hours, nor should sexual harassment be tolerated at any time. In light of the "Tailhook" scandal, you can bet that rule is now being enforced.

President Clinton is not urging a change in what is acceptable behavior. His position is that a soldier's behavior, not his or her sexual orientation, should be the test. And it is wrong to ban or discharge an individual who has not violated the behavior code.

President Clinton, in trying to fulfill his campaign promise to lift the ban on gays in the military, is maneuvering through a political minefield. He faces opposition from Gen. Colin Powell and the other Joint Chiefs, as well as from Sam Nunn, the chairman of the Senate Armed Services Committee.

Despite this opposition, gay-rights activists and others want Clinton to issue an executive order immediately and not delegate resolution of this matter to Defense Secretary Les Aspin. In an editorial, The *New York Times* accused the Joint Chiefs of being "defiantly opposed, almost to the point of insubordination."

Such give-'em-hell language is rare for the *New York Times* and regrettably advocated at a time when, if the president's proposal has any chance of being accepted, cooler heads must prevail. I support lifting the ban, but Powell and Nunn are voicing fears that need to be addressed. They believe that allowing gays and lesbians in the military to go public about their sexual orientation will destroy morale and discipline, hurt recruiting and increase the risk of AIDS among heterosexual soldiers.

It is not adequate to counter such arguments by asking, as the *New York Times'* editorial did, "Who's in charge of the military?" The questions raised have to be rationally discussed and disposed of, just as they were when comparable questions were raised by the public in 1948 when President Truman issued the executive order integrating black soldiers into regular Army units.

If the president were simply to issue an executive order, Congress could pass a law reversing him—and a majority of the Congress currently opposes lifting the ban. Doesn't logic demand that efforts be made to educate and persuade members of Congress and the military to the president's point of view?

For example, the fear of AIDS is a legitimate one. Does anyone believe there are no homosexual soldiers or IV drug users currently serving in the military? Of course not. Whatever precautionary safety measures are employed in the private sector, where medical workers encounter homosexuals and IV drug users every day, should be employed in the armed forces. Many people do not know that of all the NATO nations, only Great Britain, Greece, Turkey and the United States prohibit homosexuals from serving in the armed forces. It would be helpful to know what effect this has, if any, on the military operations of our allies.

Opponents of lifting the ban are entitled to raise their arguments. President Clinton and Secretary Aspin are not wavering if they take time to listen and persuade. People can and do change. Sen. Nunn once opposed integration and abortion. Today, he is a leader in the fight for those causes.

Gay activists often remind their opponents that one of the greatest generals of all time, Alexander the Great, was homosexual. It is also claimed that Richard the Lion-Hearted was gay, but the militants say that about everybody.

(1/29/93)

Gay Pride

This past Sunday, 250,000 gays and lesbians marched down Fifth Ave. in the Gay Pride Parade. There were few protesters. Next year, there will be fewer still.

This year's parade illustrates how far gays and lesbians have come politically. When I as mayor marched in that parade, I was scorned for doing so. But this year, the two leading candidates running for mayor, David Dinkins and Rudy Giuliani, both marched. They weren't worried about electoral fallout because there won't be any. Indeed, if they hadn't marched, it would have been a political mark against them.

When I took office in 1978, I immediately fulfilled one of my campaign pledges by issuing an executive order ending discrimination in government based on sexual orientation; with respect to employment and housing Governor Cuomo subsequently did the same. I was reelected twice after taking that action, and so was Governor Cuomo.

It took years of wrangling, but in 1986 the City Council finally passed the bill which I signed into law giving similar protections to those in the private sector. But homosexuals still lack those protections statewide because the state legislature continues to drag its feet.

This year the Democrat-controlled state assembly has finally passed the gay rights bill, which had languished there for twenty-three years, but the Republican-controlled state senate continues to lag behind. As one senate official told the *New York Post* this week, "I think it's virtually certain we'll leave for the summer without" passing the bill. "There are too many other things pending for us to do gay rights."

What are the Republican lawmakers afraid of? When I signed the gay rights law in New York City, there were those who, like Chicken Little, cried, "The sky is falling." At the time I said that a year from now, everyone will ask, "What was the ruckus all about?"

The same will hold true if the legislature has the courage—and the desire—to pass this bill.

Even in Ireland, lawmakers last week recognized the need to change with the times. As Reuters reported, "Homosexuality is coming out of the closet in Ireland. The Irish parliament yesterday ignored the protests of both the Catholic church and public opinion polls in passing a bill making homosexual relationships legal for anyone over seventeen. The law leaves homosexuals 'free to come to terms with their own lives,' said Justice Minister Maire Goeghegan Quinn." President Clinton should demonstrate the same courage as the Irish politicians. Clinton was right to make reversing the ban on gays and lesbians in the military one of his earliest priorities after taking office.

Regrettably, it gave his political opponents the ammunition they needed to sandbag the rest of his agenda.

While I believe there should not be any distinction made between the required conduct of heterosexual and homosexual soldiers, the discussions of the last six months have made it clear that some compromise is necessary before the president issues his executive order. The opposition of Sen. Sam Nunn (D-Ga.) and Gen. Colin Powell, who have the political support to get Congress to reverse such an order, cannot be ignored.

Given this political reality, I favor the policy proposed by Rep. Barney Frank (D-Mass.). Under his plan, recruiters will not ask potential soldiers about their sexual orientation (this has already been put into practice by the armed services and the Clinton administration) and soldiers will not display their sexual orientation while on duty. Off duty, you're on your own so long as you don't frighten the horses. As Clinton has made clear, it should be conduct, not orientation, on which judgments are made.

Dick Cheney, President Bush's secretary of defense, very able and highly admired by conservatives and liberals alike, said two years ago that the Pentagon policy that considers homosexuals a security risk was "a bit of an old chestnut." If he, a conservative, had had the courage to change the situation, it would have been easier and more readily accepted.

President Clinton and Secretary of Defense Les Aspin, both moderate Democrats but far more liberal than their Republican predecessors, should not flinch from their duty to correct a great injustice.

(7/2/93)

Rudolph Giuliani

The time has come to make a decision in the mayoral race. From the point of view of the city's best interest, the choice is clear.

Four years ago, David Dinkins beat me in the Democratic primary fair, square and hugely. I supported him in the general election, since we had mutually agreed that whoever won the primary would be supported by the other. I kept my word and campaigned for him throughout the city.

He has said on several occasions that without my support he could not have beaten Rudy Giuliani. His margin of victory was only 2 percent. I supported him because he was a fellow Democrat who had won the party primary.

Four years later, I have concluded that party loyalty cannot obscure the fact that David Dinkins has failed as mayor of the city of New York.

The raison d'être for his victory was stated in his own words: "My mere election will change race relations in this town." His statement did come true, but in a most unfortunate way. Race relations got worse. This town is racially polarized to an extraordinary extent, as it has never been before.

In August 1989 when I was mayor, a New York Newsday poll found that only 2 percent of New Yorkers perceived race relations as a major problem. In 1993, four years later, the *New York Times* reported that "67 percent described race relations as poor."

Who is responsible? If I were still mayor, surely David Dinkins and his supporters would hold me personally accountable. His gorgeous mosaic has been relegated to the dust bin of political rhetoric.

Mayor Dinkins presides over an administration in utter disarray. He has a far greater interest in ceremony than he has for meeting with his commissioners. Instead of engaging in hands-on government, he governs at arms' length.

Indeed, he has so distanced himself from the details of city affairs that he is unable to remove his first deputy mayor, who was extensively criticized in the Department of Investigation report on the Parking Violations Bureau. Dinkins knows that if he took such an action, the government would come to a halt because he doesn't have a clue.

What is lacking at City Hall is a sense of leadership that inspires. The latest example of the mayor's failure to lead was his reaction to the murder of Police Officer John Williamson in Washington Heights. After that officer was struck on the head and killed, the crowd cheered. The mayor's immediate response? He suspended the special towing program.

Apparently mob rule can prevail in New York City, as it did when Mayor Dinkins refused to enforce a State Supreme Court order protecting the Korean grocer in Flatbush. As it did again in Crown Heights when the police failed to protect the Jewish community from the mob and the mayor took no action for thirty-six hours. The mayor, once again, was paralyzed.

Four years ago, during one of our primary debates, Dinkins used an old Italian proverb to describe my administration: "The fish stinks from the head," he said.

I am confident history will judge my administration more kindly. We cannot wait for historians to judge the Dinkins administration because it has adversely affected our lives for four years and, if he is reelected, the quality of our lives will continue to deteriorate.

On his record, David Dinkins simply does not deserve reelection. We cannot live in an ungoverned city.

What is the alternative? Rudy Giuliani! He is not a perfect vessel, but I have concluded he is able and intelligent and has energy (the latter a missing Dinkins ingredient). Rudy Giuliani will preside over an efficient, technocratic government dedicated to delivering service and, above all, setting a single standard for all citizens.

I believe Giuliani will do what is required to insure the safety of all of us on the streets of the city and in all our communities equally, in contrast to David Dinkins, who averted his gaze while mobs engaged in violence against others who did not look like them.

At the least, Rudy Giuliani will bring a fresh commitment and a sense of fairness—one standard for one city. And if we are luckier still, he will achieve some modicum of greatness.

It's time to try a fresh fish.

(10/15/93)

* * *

As Rudy Giuliani takes office today, he has the support and good will of most New Yorkers. Surely a majority of those who voted against him want his administration to succeed for their own sake and that of the city.

The new mayor will quickly find this support is ephemeral. In ninety days he will be standing alone, winning and losing support issue by issue. The mayor has no permanent partners. His allies will change depending on the issue—and the time of day.

Over the last four years New York City has been in free fall. Recently, 42 percent of New Yorkers polled said they would move out if given a choice. Rudy can help keep them here by being candid, setting realistic goals and generating energy and excitement.

The mayor can instill confidence by holding town hall meetings in each of the city's communities. In my twelve years I had

135 local meetings. Some were heated, even raucous. For several of the more potentially explosive gatherings, the police assigned to me insisted that I wear a bullet-proof vest. I did. The mayor can never cede the streets or any public place to the predators or the rioters. He must never cancel an appearance because of security concerns.

Rudy can improve morale among city employees by regularly meeting with his commissioners and their top twenty-five people, urging them to express candidly their aspirations and tell him their problems.

The mayor has to know more about city issues than the reporters who will question him daily. If they sense he is not informed or is reluctant to face them, they will react like piranha. Rudy should answer press questions on policy matters himself, not through his press secretary.

While the mayor should take on other elected public officials with vigorous language when required, his press aides should never take it upon themselves to question the motives of those officials. If Rudy feels he has been unfairly criticized, he should try to educate the public with respect to the truth and never allow his silence to be perceived as assent.

Every mayor needs a priority issue. Mine was housing. I suggest Rudy make his the health of the city's children. He should institute a program providing free medical care at already existing city clinics and municipal hospitals for all children, from cradle to first grade, regardless of income eligibility.

Two staff agencies are vital to any mayor's success: The Office of Management and Budget and the corporation counsel. OMB guards the treasury and is responsible for keeping the city solvent and using the city's limited resources to best advantage. The corporation counsel protects the city from those scheming to rip it off. These departments should be protected from attrition and layoffs.

The mayor must demonstrate his concern for the police officers and firefighters who are on the front lines every day. His presence at their hospital bedsides when they have been injured in the line of duty means more to them than speeches. When cops are accused of brutality, he should assume they acted professionally, unless that presumption is refuted by credible evidence made available to him.

Rudy must be prepared to fire incompetent and corrupt employees expeditiously. The corrupt should be publicly discharged and their crimes referred to law enforcement. The inadequate should be required to resign, but without suffering public disgrace.

There will be those who will seek to divide the city racially by criticizing the mayor's every appointment and action. If he has been fair in his selection process, enthusiastically encouraging the disparate citizens of this city to apply and then picking the best applicant for a particular job, he shouldn't give a second thought to the yammering of those who would use race as a bludgeon to accumulate power.

Mayor Giuliani should never allow racial, ethnic or gender quotas to be used in hiring, purchasing, contracting or in any other city program. He should immediately revoke all prior mayoral executive orders which created such quotas and set-asides. Programs for the poor or for small businesses should never exclude, as his predecessor's did, those white males who are equally disadvantaged economically.

Finally, Rudy should make his first action important and symbolic. He should bring back to the mayor's office the portrait of Fiorello LaGuardia and the desk used by that great mayor, both of which were banished by former Mayor Dinkins.

(1/2/94)

Hollywood Hypocrisy

Following Colorado's passage of an anti-gay law, the beautiful people in Hollywood couldn't get to microphones fast enough to denounce Colorado and urge an economic boycott. Clutched by righteous passion, they seemed momentarily to forget their Aspen chalets. But then, as the snow began to cover the slopes, reality took over. They retreated from the boycott, saying it was unfair because it was the state of Colorado that voted for the law, not the good, parallel-skiing liberals of Aspen—they voted against it by a margin of 3-1. Pure sophistry. Barbra Streisand, who spoke out initially, now seems to be backing off from her original support of a boycott. These are the same people who boycotted South Africa on apartheid, Arizona for its lack of a Martin Luther King holiday, and Florida for its rejection of the Equal Rights Amendment. Should the need to be seen skiing in Colorado supersede one's conscience?

(12/4/92)

Homelessness

In America today, especially in New York City, there are deranged people walking the streets and sleeping on sidewalks. The city, because of straitjacket laws limiting what it can do, does nothing.

Not long ago, a proposal that many of these people should be institutionalized against their will would be called heresy by every advocate in town. I think times have changed and I have a suggestion.

The city should ask for legal authority to remove, against their will if necessary, individuals living on the streets who are diagnosed as either psychotic and likely to harm themselves or others, or suffering from a severe physical disorder requiring treatment. At present, they can only be removed if they pose a danger to themselves or others in the reasonably foreseeable future—a condition too limited in scope.

My proposal would give the city the right to place such individuals in the hospital for at least seventy-two hours. Medical personnel would then have the opportunity to examine and diagnose them thoroughly as well as wash and disinfect them.

Through such examinations, a course of treatment could be decided upon, including, where appropriate, institutionalization. Efforts could also be made to locate their families and find the individuals a place to stay, at the very least in a city shelter.

Many of you will recall the famous Billie Boggs case. In 1987, I met Billie Boggs, who was living on a grate on Second Avenue and 66th Street, lying in her own excrement. She was clearly in need of medical help.

In the early eighties, before I met Boggs, I had wanted to institute a program to treat the mentally ill homeless at hospitals. The Corporation Counsel's office advised me that legally, the city could not hospitalize individuals against their will unless they were in "imminent danger of death or bodily injury either to themselves or to others."

After encountering Boggs, I pressed the city's lawyers: "There has to be something we can do." The Corporation Counsel proposed that we could defend a more encompassing definition that would allow the city to pick up people who would be in danger "in the reasonably foreseeable future."

We created a separate unit at Bellevue to provide treatment to twenty-eight people for an average of three weeks, theoretically allowing us to treat 500 people a year. In fact, many needed more than twenty-one days on the average. Billie Boggs was one of the first people admitted to the unit.

Norman Siegel, of the New York Civil Liberties Union, had advised the homeless that they had the right to remain on the streets without treatment, so Boggs called him. The NYCLU commenced proceedings to have her discharged.

At the Court of Appeals we won the right to keep Boggs institutionalized. However, State Supreme Court Justice Irving Kirschenbaum ruled Boggs could not be compelled to take medication. So we could keep her, but not treat her.

At this point, Boggs's hospitalization was costing the city $600 a day. Bellevue is not a shelter, so the Mental Health Department notified Siegel that he could remove Boggs if he wanted to.

Boggs left Bellevue amid a crush of reporters. She became an instant celebrity, appearing in "60 Minutes,' "Donahue" and several local news programs. She was invited to lecture at Harvard Law School. When she was released she was given a job at the NYCLU office.

Shortly thereafter, she was back on the streets, shouting at passersby, and finally was arrested for drug possession and released. There's little doubt that she has returned to the streets.

Post City Hall Bureau Chief David Seifman reported in his column recently that the mayor's newly appointed commission on the homeless, headed by Andrew Cuomo, will be re-examining the Boggs case. Seifman wrote: "Three years later, there seems to be a growing sense that Koch may have been right after all."

He quoted a high-level city official as saying, "No one should be allowed to live on the sidewalk and defecate on themselves." Corporation counsel Victor Kovner said the city could ask Albany for much broader powers to conduct sweeps.

The city should do so immediately.

(9/27/91)

Harold Ickes

Harold Ickes's appointment as President Clinton's deputy chief of staff was blown out of the water last week by unsupported grand-jury leaks. Those leaks accused Ickes, a highly respected attorney who served as counsel to David Dinkins during the 1989 mayoral campaign, of perjury before a grand jury investigating the validity of a cable-television stock-transfer letter Dinkins gave his son. The *New York Times* reported: "Investigations by the United States attorney in Brooklyn and a special investigator named by the city later concluded that there was substantial evidence that the letter had been written during the campaign and backdated, and that the mayor may have lied about it, though no charges were ever brought."

Post columnist Mike McAlary wrote: "Today, there are more than a couple of prosecutors in this city who believe that the only thing separating Harold Ickes Jr. and a jail cell is his ability to go strong and silent in the face of tough questions."

I was so appalled by the leaks (remember, Ickes was never indicted) that I wrote to the acting U.S. attorney, Mary Jo White, urging that every member of her staff with knowledge of these grand jury proceedings be asked about the leaks under oath. She replied that she had referred the matter to the Department of Justice's Office of Professional Responsibility.

The appropriate action would be to prosecute anyone in or out of government who broke the law by leaking classified information, including the staff of the U.S. attorney's office.

(1/22/93)

Immigration

Nearly 300 Chinese recently arrived in America on a ship—ironically called the *Golden Venture*—which ran aground on a Queens beach. The inhumane conditions on that vessel approached those experienced by slaves who were brought by way of the "middle passage" to America from Africa.

These Chinese, and thousands like them, come of their own free will, indenturing themselves for years to pay passage fees of up to $30,000 to Chinatown gangs. Once here, they work at low-level jobs at below minimum wage and live packed in flophouses. If they fail to pay the gangs, they face being kidnaped, tortured and even murdered. Twenty or more ships with similar human cargoes are now on the high seas, headed here.

All Americans must feel for these people—especially those of us who are themselves recent immigrants, or descendants of immigrants. I'm the son of Polish Jewish immigrants who came to the U.S. in the early 1900s, fleeing poverty and discrimination. Like many others, I'm deeply sympathetic to the huge numbers of people looking to come here today to escape suffering and poverty in their own lands.

But as a country, we cannot afford to have a total open-door policy without any restrictions on entry.

Massive numbers of people throughout the world have not been disabused of the notion that the streets of America are paved with gold. It seems that most of them, given the option, would like to live here.

Wouldn't you if you were starving in Africa or Asia? Or just getting by in dreary Eastern Europe? Or if you were an Arab in France, discriminated against civilly and economically?

The Chinese describe themselves as political refugees. Many base that claim on China's strict population laws, which allow them to have only one child. But if we accept them as bonafide political refugees for that reason, doesn't it follow that people living in countries where abortion is illegal (such as Ireland and Poland) should also receive political asylum? After all, their country's policy is forcing them to give birth to unwanted children.

Many of the self-described "political refugees" who come here make stopovers in other countries on their way to the U.S., in places where they would be free to have as many children as they want. But they choose to continue on to the U.S. Why? Because it is more economically attractive.

More than 100,000 aliens applied for asylum in the U.S. from October 1991 to September 1992. Dozens more arrive daily at Kennedy Airport carrying forged papers, or no documentation at all, uttering the magic words "political asylum" as they step off the plane. The overwhelming majority are released, given permission to work and told to return for a hearing four months down the road. Eighty-five percent are never again seen by the authorities.

Unless they can immediately demonstrate a credible fear of persecution, why shouldn't these people be returned at once to the country from which they embarked—whether it be their home country or a stopover point—at the expense of the airline that brought them? All appeals would then be made from the country to which they have been returned.

Under the expanded quota designated by the Immigration Act of 1990 effective this year, 800,000 permanent immigrants will be allowed to enter the U.S. Approximately 250,000 more will come in under special programs, including 120,000 seeking political asylum. Those are generous numbers. It is not racist to believe we cannot accept millions more who are economic, not political, refugees.

Just look at Western Europe, which has no policy that allows regular immigration, but does have a history of granting asylum to political refugees. As a result, huge numbers of people not entitled to it are seeking political asylum there. This has led to rising xenophobia and violence. Countries such as Germany and France are passing new laws to limit the numbers.

There are generous-to-a-fault Americans who would end *all* restrictions on entry. This "generosity" costs them nothing. But what about the millions of poor in this country who desperately need assistance and services to help bring them out of poverty? Shall they go to the back of the line? And shall those who have made a dramatic illegal entry, who would normally not be entitled to government assistance, or even entry itself, be put at the front?

(6/17/93)

*   *   *

Every now and then, the phrase made famous by Yogi Berra, "It's déjà vu all over again," is demonstrated to a fare-thee-well. This time it applies to Congress's failure to staunch the flow of illegal immigrants into this country. It continues 365 days a year like a never-ending tidal wave.

The public was outraged last spring by a CBS "60 Minutes" report concerning illegal aliens applying for political asylum. In a one year period, 100,000 illegal aliens applied for asylum nationwide, 9,100 at JFK Airport alone. Many of these asylum seekers carried forged papers, or no documentation at all. The overwhelming majority were released, given permission to work and told to return for a hearing four months later. Eighty-five percent disappeared into the night, never to be heard from again.

The cost to state governments is enormous. This week, Florida sued the federal government for more than $1 billion in reimbursement for federally mandated services to illegal immigrants. Governor Cuomo, who is considering joining the suit, estimates such services cost New York state $970 million last year. California, with nearly one million illegals in just Los Angeles, estimates its annual costs to be more than $2 billion.

Following last year's "60 Minutes" program, I wrote to all the members of the House and Senate Judiciary Committees and the House Committee on Government Operations, asking them what action they intended to take. I received approximately fifteen responses, with most stating they would either be introducing legislation or monitoring the situation.

A year later, I again wrote to the fifty-three members of the House and Senate Judiciary Committees inquiring as to why no legislation has been passed. I received seven responses. Sen. Strom Thurmond suggested I contact the chairman of the subcommittee having jurisdiction over immigration, Sen. Ted Kennedy, and the ranking Republican, Sen. Alan Simpson.

Sen. Kennedy doesn't bother answering his mail. Sen. Simpson replied, "Senator Kennedy—and the Administration, I assume—have decided not to move that legislation. They apparently believe they can do whatever is necessary by regulation alone."

U.S. Rep. Romano Mazzoli, chairman of the House Subcommittee, summed up his frustration: "I wish I could tell you that major reforms are on the eve of enactment, but that does not appear to be the case."

Term limitations for Congress may be the only appropriate response to their inertia.

To their credit, Immigration and Naturalization officials at JFK have been able to reduce the number of asylum seekers entering the country by approximately 30 percent. But as of February, according to news reports, there was a backlog nationwide of 364,000 asylum applications, growing at a rate of 10,000 per month. Last year 18,110 claims were denied and 5,105 were approved.

Most of those claiming asylum don't bother to go through the existing process and never show up for their hearing. From October '93 to February '94, 1,046 deportation surrender orders were issued. Only one hundred aliens surrendered and very few were actually removed from the United States. It's incomprehensible that the one superpower left in the world seems to lack the moral authority to enforce its own laws.

The solution isn't just additional, costly detention facilities. What is required is legislation to stop the abuse of the political-asylum provision—proposed federal regulations don't go far enough. One sure way to have an impact on the situation is for the United States to send immediately back to the country from which they embarked those who cannot make a credible claim of political persecution—with their fare to be paid by the airline that brought them. Any appeals could be taken from abroad.

Our immigration laws are among the most generous in the world, allowing more than one million people to enter annually. Legitimate claims of political persecution should be compassionately responded to, but, regrettably, applicants abuse the process, and existing laws and judicial interpretations add to the problems.

For example, five years ago, President Bush ordered that Chinese be considered eligible for political aslyum because their government only allows them one child. In two recent cases, political asylum was granted to a Nigerian who feared her young daughters would be subject to circumcision in her homeland, and to a homosexual Mexican who said he was beaten and raped by Mexican police officers because of his sexual orientation.

Last month, a ship off the coast of Virginia unloaded one hundred Chinese illegals. According to the *New York Times,* federal officials "fear its arrival may be the first in a spring and summer wave of ships laden with immigrants headed for New York City." Why not? Our Congress is out to lunch.

(4/15/94)

Israel

During my recent trip to Israel, I discovered that the country had transformed itself. It has gone from the garrison state on constant alert that I encountered on my last visit in late 1990, to an exuberant, outgoing society looking to the future with great confidence.

Apprehension has virtually disappeared. The economy is booming, some say as the result of the newborn confidence and the ongoing privatization of Israel's formerly socialized economy. The dream is—and it's attainable from what I observed—that within five years Israel will rival the so-called economic tigers of the Pacific Rim: Japan, Singapore, Korea, Hong Kong and Taiwan.

Years of service in a variety of government offices have been a great teacher for Israel's current leadership, as I discovered in my meetings with them, and the country is reaping the benefit. Israel's president, Ezer Weizman, a war hero, is a tonic to the national psyche. Unlike his immediate predecessor, he is totally candid, has a terrific, occasionally profane sense of humor and is a throwback to what Israel was in its earliest days. He is unencumbered by traditional diplomatic niceties.

The prime minister, Yitzhak Rabin, is still restrained but no longer dour and taciturn. He exudes self-confidence along with a willingness to listen and take reasonable chances in the nation's quest for peace.

The foreign minister, Shimon Peres, is no longer facile and pedantic, but is now a statesman with vision. His goal is a tripartite confederation made up of Israel, the Palestinians and Jordan.

Most intriguing was the young Israeli, Commander R., whom I met. Thirty-four and a lieutenant colonel in the air force, he is a fifteen-year veteran in charge of a squadron. He and his wife, D., were born on separate kibbutzim and now have two children. They are a highly intelligent and sophisticated couple with an unexpected gentleness. Willing to make every sacrifice for their nation, including their lives, they clearly want an honorable peace with their Arab neighbors and will support the reasonable compromises needed to achieve it.

Ariel Sharon, the one-time defense minister, is still very active. His peace plan for the West Bank severely limits Palestinian autonomy, giving greater protection to Israel's security by retaining all of the high terrain. Others commenting on his proposal agreed with it—but conveyed with a smirk or shrug that it is fantasy to believe that the Palestinians would accept it.

Teddy Kollek, now eighty-three, has been mayor of Jerusalem for twenty-six years and, having first said that he wouldn't run, is now campaigning for another term. His friends worry that he will be defeated because of age, longevity and the expectation that he will step down to make way for a hand-picked successor instead of serving a full term. Jerusalem is Teddy's city; it will never be the same without him. If it can be said that anyone deserves a last hurrah, it's Teddy.

I was in Israel at the invitation of the mayor of Tel Aviv, Cheech Lahat, a most generous host. He is stepping down after being in office for twenty years. If he were to run, he would win reelection by acclamation, having changed a sleepy town into a cultural and economic colossus. His personality and achievements are the pride of the city. He outraged a few when he denounced as "deserters" the male citizens of Tel Aviv who left town when the SCUD missiles arrived, but he endeared himself to the rest of the country and, of course, to those who stayed.

Lahat invited me to his city to witness the naming of a street in my honor, a distinction given by Tel Aviv to only fifteen people during their lifetimes. Several years ago he had sought to so honor me, but was unable to secure the required consent of 66 percent of the people who lived and worked on the street he selected.

This time, he said at the ribbon-cutting, there was no problem because, "I picked a street on which there were no residents or workers." To comfort me, he added, "Ed, don't feel badly. Remember, in Israeli elections the government can't even get the support of 51 percent of the residents and workers."

I am indeed grateful to Lahat for the honor bestowed upon me.

(8/20/93)

The Israel Day Parade

Painful as it is for me to do so, I will be boycotting the Salute to Israel Parade this Sunday for the second year in a row.

Last year, for the first time in decades, I would not march because the sponsors had barred the Beth Simchat Torah synagogue, a predominantly gay and lesbian congregation, from marching behind its own banner. This year, the discrimination continues under a new guise.

In an attempt to avoid public controversy—but accomplish their same goal of exclusion—those same organizers have come up with a new, but transparent, scheme: Bar all adults from the body of the parade, and permit only children from Jewish parochial schools to march in separate contingents. In the past, various adult groups, such as the Jewish War Veterans, marched under their own banners.

Under the 1994 regulations, only those Jewish schools with seventy-five or more children would be entitled to march separately. Beth Simchat Torah has only twenty-five enrolled students, so they would have to go to the back of the bus: No separate contingent, no separate banner.

The ultra-Orthodox leaders in charge will not countenance a congregation whose spiritual leader, a duly ordained rabbi, is lesbian. They will not permit that congregation, hospitable to homosexuals and lesbians, to march, depriving Israel of their public support.

I was invited by the organizations to march at the head of this Sunday's Salute to Israel Parade as a grand marshal, and then received a follow-up call asking for a confirmation. I said to the caller, "But you've changed the parade rules and don't want adults, just children." The reply: "Not exactly. We want dignitaries at the head of the parade, and we want you to lead them."

I replied, "But the change is really a device to eliminate Beth Simchat Torah congregants from marching separately." He said, "Only partly." Not wanting to lend myself to such chicanery, I declined the honor.

Those familiar with the controversy surrounding the Irish Lesbian and Gay Organization (ILGO) and the St. Patrick's Day Parade may ask how this situation differs. The Salute to Israel is primarily secular, whereas the St. Patrick's Day Parade is overwhelmingly religious. No advocacy banners, not even pro-life banners, are allowed at the St. Patrick's Day Parade. The lone exception is the unifying motto "England Out of Ireland." There's no question that ILGO, by seeking to march separately as gays and lesbians, wanted to engage in advocacy.

In the Salute to Israel Parade, Congregation Beth Simchat Torah sought no advocacy banner. The congregation simply wanted to display a banner bearing its name, as all other synagogues do. That banner in no way conveys the sexual orientation of the people marching behind it, who, by the way, include hererosexuals as well as homosexuals who support the State of Israel.

It is an outrage that Beth Simchat Torah cannot march under it's own banner. It ill becomes the Jewish community to discriminate against Jews based on their sexual orientation and, even worse, to discriminate against Jewish children by requiring the artificial number of seventy-five to prohibit them from marching as a separate unit. What conceivable justification is there for discriminating against these children?

Regrettably, Jews and Israel have too few friends in this world. For Jews themselves to create ridiculous and arbitrary exclusionary rules in a parade honoring Israel, regulations that further divide Jews based on their sexual orientation, is counterproductive to both Israel and the Jewish community here in New York City.

Of course, this is not a monumental issue, but, nevertheless, it is important as a human rights matter. Do we speak up now, or do we wait until the ultra-Orthodox demand that homosexual Jews be barred from citizenship in Israel under the Law of Return?

In Israel, the Orthodox rabbinate, with the consent of the Israeli government, has prohibited rabbis affiliated with the Conservative and Reform branches from performing marriages for their congregants. The rabbinate, and the State of Israel, have also barred civil marriages. As a result, many native born Israelis, as well as recent Russian and Ethiopian immigrants, admitted under the Law of Return, who are not able to convince the rabbinate they are bona fide Jews, must go to Cyprus to marry, or obtain a proxy mail-order marriage from Paraguay.

It's shameful that the Israeli government allows this harassment of Jews who are either Conservative, Reform or without affiliation. Just as outrageous are the artifices used by the Salute to Israel Parade sponsors in excluding Jews.

In the words of Phil Ochs' great song of protest, "I ain't marchin' anymore."

(5/20/94)

Leonard Jeffries

The violence and anti-Semitism in Crown Heights has pushed CUNY Prof. Leonard Jeffries out of the headlines. But his anti-white, anti-Semitic rhetoric can't be ignored, especially because some well-known and respected people are continuing to defend him.

Daily News columnist Juan Gonzalez defended Jeffries in a recent column, saying anti-Semitic and anti-Italian remarks taken from Jeffries's July speech were just "a few snippets from a speech." Gonzalez added that people should not be "calling for his academic scalp without talking to the man or examining his theories."

What are some of those theories? That "rich Jews" were responsible for the slave trade; that the African "sun people" are humane and the European "ice people" are not, and that the skin pigment melanin makes blacks mentally superior to whites.

Gonzalez wrote, "You may disagree with Jeffries after listening to him, but the man has done extensive scholarship on world and African history. In fact, throughout the speech, Jeffries held up book after book by other scholars, many of them white, to buttress his arguments."

Does Gonzalez feel that we should also seriously examine the racial theories of the Ku Klux Klan for nuggets of truth? Should we study the doctrine of David Duke, the former imperial wizard of the Ku Klux Klan, because he is well read and can produce literature supporting his racist views?

Gonzalez went on to say that Jeffries occasionally may generalize "and say things that can be construed as anti-Semitic and anti-white," but that "Malcolm X, much admired in the grave . . . also voiced anti-white views in his early years. But Malcolm's thoughts evolved." Malcolm X did refute his earlier anti-white statements and is now deservedly venerated. Jeffries cannot be so admired, because he continues to spew his racism with enthusiasm.

There is an amazing difference between the reaction of white leaders and the reaction of many black leaders in this matter. Of course, there are white racists like CUNY Prof. Michael Levin, but they are overwhelmingly denounced by both whites and blacks. That's not the case when a black individual like Jeffries engages in comparable racial rhetoric. In Jeffries's case, what's missing are denunciations from most black leaders. Too often there is leaden silence or support for his views.

Applying special rules to black bigots was demonstrated this week by the New York state chapter of the NAACP. In an apparent reference to Jeffries's racial pronouncements, it passed a banal resolution which said, "It is our belief that no useful purpose can be served by launching assaults on any one racial, religious or ethnic group." But the resolution did not say that those "assaults" were perpetrated by Jeffries on whites, nor did it condemn him by name. Why not? Was the NAACP's condemnation of David Duke treated the same way?

Gonzalez pointed out that Jeffries's speech was almost two hours long. Undoubtedly, some non-racist facts crept in. He is not being attacked for those statements, but rather for his over-all racist point of view. Even Hitler—and Jeffries should not be equated with Hitler—spoke some words of truth. He said that the Versailles Treaty imposed on Germany after World War I was unfair—and that was true. Does that true statement sanitize his volumes of vitriol?

On Sunday I watched "Sunday Edition," the show I once cohosted on channel 2. (They fired me because they said I was too controversial; I am now a commentator on Channel 5.) Jim Jensen and Ernest Tollerson, editorial-page editor at *New York Newsday*, two people who usually show intelligence and good judgment, disgraced themselves by trying to excuse Jeffries's racism and anti-Semitism. They sought to convey that the balance of his message on multiculturalism was more important than his views on race and that we should not be diverted by the occasional lapses in his rhetoric—in effect, Gonzalez's "snippets" reference.

Paraphrasing Gertrude Stein: A bigot is a bigot is a bigot, no matter the color of his skin.

(8/23/91)

Ed Koch

Using the words of Norman Mailer, this column can be aptly titled "Advertisements for Myself."

My parents came here as Polish Jewish immigrants, and this country and this city have given their son perhaps much more than that son deserved. Early on, I had the opportunity to run against a national political figure, Carmine DeSapio, and I won. From that point on, my political rise was meteoric.

I was elected to the City Council, the first Democrat from my district in thirty-eight years. I became a congressman unexpectedly—defeating the scion of one of the major Republican families, Whitney North Seymour Jr., to become the first Democrat to hold that seat in thirty-one years. I thought to myself, "How can a guy with two names beat a guy with four?"

And, of course, the highlight of my political career was serving as mayor of New York City for three terms.

There are only two other mayors in the modern era who served twelve years—Fiorella LaGuardia and Robert Wagner. There is now a library at LaGuardia Community College containing the works of the three of us.

Prior to being elected to Congress, I was senior partner in the small law firm of Koch Lankenau Schwartz & Kovner, which produced one mayor and two city corporation counsels in twelve years. On January 1, 1990, I returned to the law, becoming a partner in the firm of Robinson Silverman Pearce Aronsohn & Berman.

Over the course of the last thirty years, I have basically kept the same friends, adding a few from time to time. My relationships with my sister and brother and their families are very close, and I see them for dinner or a movie at least once a week.

My health is excellent—notwithstanding the fact that I take six pills every morning, from aspirin to Zantac. How many sixty-eight-year-old men go to the gym and exercise intensely for an hour a day with a personal trainer? Very few. When I had my stroke almost six years ago, the examining doctor said I had the brain of a twenty-eight-year-old. When I had my pacemaker inserted a little over a year ago, that doctor said I had the body of a forty-two-year-old. I'm now trying to bring brain and body into closer alignment.

As a result of my labors, my financial resources have never been better. I even have a housekeeper and, yes, she is an American citizen. I'm one of those rare people who pays "on the books," including Social Security taxes. No, I'm not interested in being attorney general.

So, how do I spend my time? I practice law. I write this weekly column. I host a daily talk-radio program on WABC-AM, from 11 a.m. to noon, that's the second-highest rated in the time slot out of the forty-five AM and FM stations. My handle is "The Voice of Reason," which I've copyrighted, so I'm the only Voice of Reason in the United States.

I write movie reviews that appear in the *Manhattan Spirit, Our Town* and other local papers. I do commercials: Remember Slim Fast and my losing 40 pounds? I lecture around the country. I teach at NYU. I have just written my fifth book, *Citizen Koch*, and am collaborating on a play I hope will be staged on Broadway.

The nicest thing that happens to me every day is people walking up to me and saying, "Oh, Mayor, you must run again." And I respond, "No, the people threw me out, and now the people must be punished." Almost invariably, they respond, "Mayor, we've been punished. How long?"

One of my additional pleasures in life comes from the fact that many of my fiercest critics in the media—who took pleasure in attacking me, often unfairly—have gone into oblivion, while here I am part of the media. I never said I was a nice guy.

Shortly after I left office, I was on an elevator with TV newsman Doug Johnson and he said, "Now you're one of us," and I replied, "Now that I'm one of us it doesn't mean I have to like us."

I never would have believed that things would go so well after I left the mayoralty. But as my mother would have said, don't give yourself *aynhoreh* (the evil eye). My cup runneth over. Allah Akbar.

(2/12/93)

Leaving Gracie Mansion

New Year's Eve was my last night at Gracie Mansion. About sixty people attended the party I held.

There were commissioners from my prior administrations and from my last one, as well as friends—old and new—all of whom had been involved with the city in one way or another.

The thought entered my mind, and I mentioned it jocularly, that some there might be tempted to take with them some inconsequential memento, such as an ashtray, since many of the guests might well never return to Gracie Mansion. But we do not have many ashtrays at the Mansion.

Wine glasses, which had the seal of the city printed on them, used to be considered fair game for the thousands of guests who came through Gracie Mansion. So we replaced them with ones that had no seals, and they lost their appeal as mementos.

Overnight guests never took things. Can you imagine people like Menachem Begin or Jacques Chirac, the former French premier, stealing towels?

But while I myself packed my last things that morning, I thought to myself: What will happen to these exceedingly nice Ralph Lauren towels? I have used them every day, and they are at least six years old. Undoubtedly the Mansion will purchase new towels for Mayor and Mrs. Dinkins. The old towels will go unused, except perhaps by an occasional guest. The thought entered my mind: Who would care if I took two towels as mementos? Isn't taking hotel towels the great American swindle? But in the end, I left them on the rack.

At about one A.M., the last guest departed and, true to my word, I left for my new apartment. My friends Victor and Lee Botnick went with me to see if they could be helpful. And they were. Lee showed me how to use the new coffee machine with a timer—a type which probably didn't exist twelve years ago, when I last lived in a private dwelling.

On New Year's Day, I woke up in my new apartment and, lo and behold, the aroma of freshly brewed coffee was in the air. Then I showered. When I went to dry myself, the only towels on the rack were three small dish towels. Have you ever tried drying yourself with dish towels? It is not pleasant—I thought longingly of those two Ralph Lauren towels hanging on the rack at the Mansion.

(1/12/90)

Multiculturalism

There is currently a firestorm raging in this country regarding the way we teach our kids history. The result: a call for a new multiculturalism that seeks to rewrite history.

The latest chapter concerns a report issued this week by an advisory committee appointed by New York State Commissioner of Education Thomas Sobol. The report recommends that the state's social-studies curricula be culturally inclusive and be infused with a multicultural perspective.

The report is gobbledygook seeking to denigrate our accepted common history, with its roots in the original English, Spanish and French settlement of the United States. Should we be rewriting history just to make people feel good? That's not history; that's psychiatry.

Why should we apologize for being Eurocentric? This is our overall common tradition. Of course, many groups have contributed to the fabric that is America. But the reality is the early settlers were Europeans, and Americans share a common heritage of cultural values, language and tradition that is overwhelmingly based on our English and European roots.

It is fatuous to seek to convey that every group around the world at every stage significantly contributed to the creation of America. For example, I regret to say there were no Jews on the Mayflower. But a fact is a fact. And Christopher Columbus was Italian, not Puerto Rican; he discovered Puerto Rico . . . excuse me, I mean he landed there; Puerto Rico was already occupied by the Indians . . . excuse me, I mean Native Americans.

Noted historian Arthur Schlesinger Jr., who withdrew from the panel last fall but continues as a consultant, has written an impressive dissent to the report in which he says: "The ethnic interpretation, moreover, reverses the historic theory of America—which has been, not the preservation and sanctification of old cultures and identities, but the creation of a new national culture and a new national identity. As Secretary of State John Quincy Adams told a German contemplating migration to these shores, those who settle in America must recognize one necessity: 'They must cast off the European skin, never to resume it. They must look forward to their posterity rather than backward to their ancestors.' "

Some proponents of multiculturalism would have us view Thomas Jefferson and George Washington not in the context of the age in which they lived, but by today's values so as to denigrate them because they owned slaves. Yet, some of those same revisionists extol ancient Egypt and its slave civilization.

There are even advocates of multiculturalism who have praised young Americans who would prefer to speak black English or keep Spanish as their daily mother tongue instead of learning to speak and use English fluently.

Too many people are afraid to speak out, to speak of America with pride, because they fear they will be accused of jingoism, racism and behavior that is not deemed politically correct. We are allowing ourselves to become subject to the fad of the day at the whim and caprice of those who have decided the American experiment has failed. It has not. Ask those who are clamoring to share the American dream by crossing our borders by the hundreds of thousands each year, legally and illegally.

As Schlesinger says in his dissent, "I would only beg them [the committee members] to consider what kind of nation we will have if we press further down the road to cultural separatism and ethnic fragmentation, if we institutionalize the classification of our citizens by ethnic and racial criteria and if we abandon our historic commitment to an American identity. What will hold our people together then?" What indeed.

We didn't all come over on the same boat, at the same time or under the same conditions; but we're in the same boat now. The proposed emphasis on a multicultural curriculum, with its endorsement of fragmentation instead of unity, may not end up simply rocking the boat, but rather sinking it.

(6/28/91)

Nuclear Power

America's energy policy is too greatly influenced by radicals, both in and out of government. An anti-nuclear energy motto summing up the goals of the radicals might read: Don't build any more nuclear-energy plants, dismantle the ones we now have, and scare the hell out of the public with the specter of an American Chernobyl.

Chernobyl, of course, was an antiquated and crude facility of a kind that isn't built in the Western world. The fact is that fossil fuels are far more dangerous than the nuclear-energy plants built in accordance with Western standards.

"Western" in this case means France, which now gets 70 percent of its electricity from nuclear power, and Japan, which gets 28 percent of its electricity from nuclear power. Japan, as it happens, is relying more heavily on nuclear power with each passing year.

The French build their nuclear-power plants on the basis of American designs. The Japanese take only five years to build their facilities. In this country, we don't use the advanced designs we sell to the French, and it takes us 11 years to build a plant—when we are allowed to do so.

Modern, standardized nuclear-power plants are safe, cheap and efficient. Relying on such plants is a good deal more responsible than using traditional fossil fuels such as oil and coal, which—as the Exxon spills in Alaska and Arthur Kill demonstrate—are manifestly harmful to the environment.

Most people don't realize that over 60 percent of our electricity is supplied by coal—the fuel that, on a daily basis, probably does the environment the greatest harm. Coal mining, moreover, is a notoriously dangerous occupation—it causes grave illnesses and often brings an early death to miners.

Most people don't know that we're steadily increasing our dependency on foreign oil. Not only does this weaken our position in world affairs, it wreaks havoc on our domestic economy. Consider that 40 percent of our trade deficit last year came from the purchase of foreign oil.

And what of the future? It is expected that by 1993, we will be importing some 50 percent of our oil from abroad.

Modern, standardized nuclear plants can be built in half the time it currently takes, if we can limit the duration of lawsuits that impede timely completion or prevent it altogether.

The ill-fated Shoreham plant on Long Island is an object lesson in what's wrong with the way we let passion prevail over reason in the making of our nuclear-energy policy.

Supported by public officials from Long Island, who were fired up and frightened by a small but effective band of environmental activists, Governor Cuomo decided that the

Shoreham plant should be shut down before it could even be opened.

As an inducement to shut the plant, the state agreed that the Long Island Lighting Co., which built Shoreham, could impose an automatic 63 percent rate increase over a ten-year period. According to Congressman Norman Lent of Nassau Country, this means consumers will pay almost $4 billion of the $5 billion it cost to build Shoreham, plus the $444 million it will cost to dismantle the plant. What a waste.

The governor, moreover, according to Representative Lent, based his estimate of the cost to Lilco customers on an unrealistically low price of oil—$14 a barrel. Actually, oil is already up to $20 a barrel. As the price climbs, so too will the automatic rate increase.

Spilled oil poisons our waters. Burning coal poisons our air and causes acid rain, which pollutes our rivers and lakes. Meanwhile, our nation's dependency on foreign governments to meet its energy needs increases at an alarming rate.

Nuclear energy could be the answer to these problems. But, based on the Shoreham experience, it appears that New York's anti-nuclear activists have won the day. The federal government is trying to prevent the actual demolition of Shoreham. Thus, the fight for nuclear power on Long Island may yet be waged again in the future—perhaps on the day when Long Islanders see their new electricity bills.

(4/6/90)

Peace

Jews worldwide, myself included, have an ongoing concern for the safety of Israel. It is the sanctuary for Jews not fortunate enough to live in lands where they have equal rights as full-fledged citizens.

Now to the signing of the peace agreement between Israel and the Palestinian Liberation Organization:

What is most significant is that the Arabs have given up the option of war and terrorism as a way to impose their point of view.

Israeli Prime Minister Yitzhak Rabin and PLO Chief Yasser Arafat have placed their lives in danger in seeking to bring peace to the people they represent.

The danger they face is from some of their own people who prefer a perpetual war, with parents weeping as their sons' and daughters' coffins are lowered into graves.

More than 17,000 Israeli soldiers have been killed in combat since 1948. If that figure were extrapolated to the American population, it would mean 850,000 dead American soldiers.

Ongoing discussions will deal with other parts of the West Bank and East Jerusalem (the latter lies outside the old walled city). There will be demands from the West Bank Jewish settlers; there will be demands by East Jerusalem Arab residents. Shimon Peres, foreign minister of Israel, envisions a tripartite confederation incorporating Jordan, West Bank/Gaza and Israel.

The East Jerusalem Arab sector can continue as part of the undivided City of Jerusalem, as well as serving as the seat of government for a new Arab entity, with Jews continuing to reside in East Jerusalem as they do now as full citizens of Israel.

If I could govern New York City with five borough presidents, Teddy Kollek can surely govern Jerusalem with one Arab borough president. Why would it be offensive for an Arab flag to fly over the borough of East Jerusalem? Surely Jerusalem can survive two flags, particularly when the Western Wall and the ancient walled city remain in the State of Israel.

Ariel Sharon and Yitzhak Shamir oppose the present peace plan, but ironically, without their prior actions it would not have been possible.

It was Sharon's success in shattering the rising might of the PLO in Lebanon with the '82 invasion that helped pave the way.

Shamir had the strength to resist the unconscionable demands of the United Nations, then the agent of Third World Arab countries and the Soviets, who were seeking to destabilize and dele-gitimize Israel.

Like the bad-cop, good-cop scenario, we see in contrast the different courage and statesmanship demonstrated by Israel's present leaders, Yitzhak Rabin and Shimon Peres, who are will-ing to take a chance for peace.

They've had to deal with the religious fanatics who believe it is a sin to give up one inch of the ancient Kingdoms of Israel and Judah. They've also had to face the security arguments of Israelis in the settlements and Israel proper.

Rabin and Arafat must learn from the assassinations of Indira Gandhi, Mahatma Gandhi and Anwar Sadat. They must be constantly aware of the dangers they face, perhaps from some-one they have trusted or even from their own security forces.

How strange it is to say on this Rosh Hashanah: "Dear God, please protect both Yitzhak Rabin and Yasser Arafat from harm."

Rabin summed it up when he quoted Ecclesiastes: "To every-thing there is a season and a time to every purpose under heaven . . . a time of war and a time of peace."

Yes, "The time for peace has come."

(9/17/93)

Personal Morality

In a discussion concerning the high rate of pregnancy among the students of New York City's public high schools, I asked a friend, "What's the rate in the Jewish parochial schools in Brooklyn?" He replied, "I can only think of one case." I said, "What happened?" He said, "They closed the school."

The public schools don't keep pregnancy rates. But according to city Health Department data, 14 percent of the births in the black community in 1991 were to mothers who were under twenty. For Puerto Ricans, 20 percent. Non-Puerto Rican Hispanics, 10 percent. Whites, 3 percent. Undoubtedly, most are school-age girls.

While the Archdiocese of New York City also does not maintain formal statistics (and I suggest that both systems change that policy), it estimates that fewer than 2 percent of girls attending its high schools become pregnant.The public high schools are largely minority, but 50 percent of the children in the Catholic high schools in Manhattan, the Bronx and Staten Island are black and Hispanic.

So why are more teenagers in the public schools sexually active? The lack of family structure and values.

Everyone knows that parents are often embarrassed and uncomfortable talking about sex to their children, so it has been necessary to use our classrooms to instruct children on sexual matters. Perhaps we should also be using those classrooms to help the parents learn how to approach this highly charged subject.

Thus far, the classrooms in our central cities, certainly New York, have done an admittedly lousy job. Long before Sen. Pat Moynihan created the seminal phrase, "defining deviancy down," our classrooms were doing exactly that with our youngsters.

Several years ago, the New York State Board of Regents, as reported in an October 1992 *New York Times* editorial, "declared that oral and written instruction on AIDS prevention must devote 'substantially more time and attention' to abstinence than to other means of avoiding infection." The *Times* in the same breath denounced this effort, saying it "needlessly, destructively interferes with a teacher's ability to frame effective courses." The *Times* believes that abstinence (remember, we are talking about children) should not be stressed or preferred over the advocacy of condoms. They see abstinence as being as outmoded as a chastity belt.

Following this view, in his last week of office, New Jersey Gov. Jim Florio unwisely vetoed legislation that would have required school districts to teach sexual abstinence as the only reliable way to prevent pregnancy and sexually transmitted diseases, including AIDS. His reason: To do so would be imposing a "political intrusion" on local school decisions. Absurd.

Would legislators, mayors or governors treat the middle-class and wealthy children of Scarsdale with the same contempt they treat minority children? They assume that the latter cannot meet the higher ethical and moral standards we expect and demand of white children living in middle-class school districts. Black and Hispanic parents and civic leaders should be demanding the same high standards for their children. They are responsible for lower standards by their silence.

Let's look at what happened in Atlanta, in a school system that is overwhelmingly black, when the educators demanded higher standards. A *Times* editorial cites an Atlanta program that trains students "to develop the social skills to resist sex . . . By the end of the eighth grade . . . only 8 percent of the boys who participated had begun having sex, compared with 29 percent of those not in the program. The impact on girls was even more striking. Only 1 percent had started having sex compared with 15 percent."

Are those black children different than those living in New Haven? Yet, in New Haven the school board recently decided that ten-year-olds in the fifth grade would be given free access to condoms. What kind of society are we creating?

I am for condoms being available, but at the high school level and with a parental opt-out provision. However, we should not accept the premise that moral values cannot be taught in our public schools while we are teaching kids how to put on a condom. Apparently, the pursuit of freedom from religion has driven moral values from our school system. It makes no sense.

Political Correctness

We have lost our common sense. Society is in the process of giving in to the extremists at every level. Racial quotas and preferential treatment are now accepted as the norm. Opponents of quotas are seen as racists.

According to the new rules, white American males have forfeited the right to compete equally for jobs with those groups in our society, minorities and women, against whom there had

• The *Murphy Brown* controversy: Quayle was derided as foolish for taking on a popular television sitcom and characterized as unfairly sitting in judgment on every mother with a child born out of wedlock.

It was brilliant—whether consciously or unconsciously—for Quayle to have invoked *Murphy Brown*. If he hadn't, would any attention have been paid to the substance of his speech? And isn't it a legitimate cause for concern that in 1989, in the United States, 19 percent of white children and 66 percent of black children were born out of wedlock? And that these numbers have grown from 11 percent and 55 percent respectively in 1980 and 6 percent and 38 percent in 1970?

The vice president was saying that the media and others are encouraging women to have children out of wedlock by glorifying single parenthood and comparing it favorably with marriage. These savants disregard the fact that these children usually stay in poverty far longer than if they had been born into an intact family. Quayle did not attack the individual woman and certainly not the child, but rather the media who make single parenthood seem like fun and games.

• The abortion controversy: Dan Quayle's caring statement regarding his daughter is being mocked by those who should know better—and who share my pro-choice view on abortion. Talk show host Larry King had the following colloquy with the vice president; King asked: "What if your daughter . . . came to you with that problem all fathers fear? How would you deal with it?" Quayle: "Well, it is a hypothetical situation. I hope that I never do have to deal with it . . . " King: "What would you do?" Quayle: "I would counsel her and talk to her and support her on whatever decision she made." King: "And if the decision was abortion, you'd support her, as a parent?" Quayle: "I'd support my daughter. I'd hope that she wouldn't make that decision."

The next day, Quayle, referring to his daughter, who is a minor of thirteen, said, "under the current situation, she would have the child." While I can't understand how parents could ever put a child of thirteen through pregnancy and childbirth, I recognize that it is a matter of personal conscience.

Quayle's answer was clear: He would advise his adult daughter against having an abortion, but would support her decision. As a caring father what should he have said? That he would insist she not have an abortion and would end his relationship with her if she did?

There were derisive comments from some. "Sounds like choice to me," said House Speaker Tom Foley. Governor Cuomo said, ". . . you can't make a distinction between your own blood and everybody else's daughter." These political figures sought to convey that Quayle had betrayed his philosophy on abortion. But Quayle simply said he would not disown his daughter. Would Cuomo, who is personally opposed to abortion and has three daughters, do otherwise?

The media has relentlessly singled Dan Quayle out for ridicule because they don't share his arch-conservative views. We deserve better from the fourth estate and the leaders in both parties.

(7/31/92)

Rap and Race

What would happen to a white rap artist if he recorded a song that degraded or threatened the lives of blacks?

If a white rapper composed such songs, the sky would fall, as it should. Public officials, clergy, columnists and civic leaders would correctly denounce such bigotry from the board room and the pulpit, from the classroom and the news room, from the halls of Congress to the City Halls of this nation.

Not all black rappers compose offensive songs, and, of course, blacks aren't alone in writing racist lyrics. But some do combine bigotry with direct calls for violence against those whom they perceive to be their enemies. Have you heard the lyrics of some leading black rappers?

In 1990, some Jewish leaders correctly assailed the rap group Public Enemy for its anti-Semitic, anti-white message. They called on CBS records not to distribute Public Enemy's record, "Welcome to the Terror Dome," which contained the lyrics: "Crucifixion ain't no fiction; so-called chosen dozen. Apology made to whatever pleases. Still they got me like Jesus . . . Backstab, grab the flag from the back of the lab, told the Rab [rabbi]: get off the rag." Chuck D, leader of group, denied the lyrics were anti-Semitic, saying they were not referring to Jews but to the media.

In 1989 Professor Griff, then a member of Public Enemy, told the *Washington Times* that Jews were responsible for "the majority of wickedness that goes on across the globe" and "have a history of killing black men." Griff also said, "The Jews can come against me. They can send their faggot little hit men," and, "Is it coincidence that the Jews run the jewelry business, and it's named Jew-elry? No coincidence." Chuck D announced that he had fired Griff, saying, "Offensive remarks by my brother Professor Griff are not in line with Public Enemy's policy."

Two months later, Griff rejoined the band with little protest outside of Jewish groups. I ask the same question of the Anti-Defamation League posed at the time: Would there be no reaction if a white racist group were targeting blacks in a similar way? Griff has also launched a solo career.

Public Enemy's latest outrage is its video, "By the Time I Get to Arizona." As the *New York Times* reported, "The video depicts the group's lead singer, Chuck D, leading a paramilitary charge, and ends with an actor portraying an Arizona governor being killed by a car bomb." Apparently, this is the group's way of protesting the fact that last year Arizona voters rejected a holiday honoring Martin Luther King Jr.'s birthday. The song is part of Public Enemy's latest album, *Apocalypse 91: The Enemy Strikes Back*. Can you believe it's been nominated for a Grammy Award?

Public Enemy is not alone in its bigotry. Rapper Ice Cube's latest album contains songs disparaging Jews and Koreans. The song "Black Korea" says: "Don't follow me up and down your market or your little chop-suey ass will be a target of a nation-wide boycott . . . So pay respect to the black fist or we'll burn your store right down to a crisp."

Incredibly, according to the *New Republic,* rap's "primary audience is white and lives in the suburbs." It brings to mind Lenin's remark, "The capitalists will sell us the rope with which we will hang them." The remark has some contemporary resonance.

Public Enemy's and Ice Cube's recent releases are direct calls for violence. Do we have to wait for violence to occur before action can be taken? Canada and many European countries have created group libel as a cause of action. We should consider such a remedy. These particular artists should be pursued criminally for inciting violence, and their bigoted, racist recordings should be boycotted by consumers.

Martin Luther King used boycotts effectively against white storekeepers who discriminated against blacks. We should take a leaf out of his book and boycott the record companies that finance and sell these racist and violent outpourings.

(1/17/92)

Republicans or Reactionaries?

I watched the opening night of the Republican Convention with revulsion. I was horrified by what I heard and saw.

Only former President Ronald Reagan deserved any respect. Now in his eighties, he reminds me, as I am sure he does most of America, of a favorite uncle who led a good life and served his country well. Yes, he had tunnel vision, but, my God, what a tunnel! He deserves credit for the peaceful collapse of the Soviet empire and the end of the Cold War. He was foolishly derided by the cognoscenti for his reference to the Soviet Union as the evil empire. Wasn't he right?

Preceding him on the podium in Houston was the blended face of mean-spiritedness and evil: a composite of Fritz Kuhn, Huey Long, Charles Lindbergh, Father Coughlin, Joe McCarthy, Roy Cohn and David Duke. Pat Buchanan reveled in the applause of putative brown-shirts who cheered his verbal bashing and threatening of their fellow citizens who are different in appearance, religion or philosophy.

The chairman of the Republican Party, Richard Bond, took us back to the days of McCarthy, telling television commentator Maria Shriver, "But we are America. These other people are not America." Remind you of our dark past?

Bond set the stage for Buchanan, who brought down the house by referring to the Democrats who attended last month's convention in New York as cross-dressers. Cleverly, and in the style of his demagogic predecessors, he was seeking to link the Democratic Party with sexual perversion. Communism is dead, so now the Democrats who were once denounced as soft on communism are to be pilloried as the Party of Perverts.

When he railed against the liberals, the radicals, the homosexuals and the feminists, bringing the delegates to their feet shouting his praises, he was following in the footsteps of Lindbergh at the notorious isolationist America First convention in 1940 at Madison Square Garden.

At this moment, the Republican Party is going through what the Democratic Party went through in 1972, when the radical-left McGovern crazies took over the party. The Republicans are now willing captives of the archradical right. Their party platform is the most reactionary put together by either party, Republican or Democratic, in living memory. Imagine advocating a constitutional amendment that would consider it a criminal act to abort a fetus even if completing the pregnancy would endanger the life of the mother. Shouldn't the woman be making the decision about whether she lives or dies? And what do you think a caring husband or the woman's young children would want? It should be their decision, not that of a prohibitive law.

What does President Bush think? He says they have their platform, he has his. Ridiculous. He's the party's standard-bearer and he carries their baggage.

Bill Bennett, former secretary of education, says in effect, "Don't worry, the amendment will never carry." That is what the German tycoons who supported Adolf Hitler said, despite *Mein Kampf*, which laid out his master plan. It did happen. Take them at their word.

Mary Fisher, the socialite who contracted AIDS from her husband, held the audience in thrall Wednesday night when she addressed the convention. She closed her remarks with Pastor Martin Niemoller's historic statement, "In Germany, they came first for the communists, and I didn't speak up because I wasn't a communist. Then they came for the Jews, and I didn't speak up because I wasn't a Jew. Then they came for the trade unionists, and I didn't speak up because I wasn't a trade unionist. Then they came for the Catholics, and I didn't speak up because I was a Protestant. Then they came for me, and by that time, no one was left to speak up."

The Buchanan Republicans are starting with the homosexuals. Who will be next? And who will speak up now? And if not now, when?

(8/21/92)

The Saint Patrick's Day Parade

When I opened the *New York Times* at 6 A.M. on March 17, I had already decided to march in the St. Patrick's Day parade, as I have been doing since the early sixties. After reading the *Times*'s editorial on the subject, I was even more convinced that my decision was the right one.

The editorial began: "The St. Patrick's Day parade in New York City is bound to be a joyless, bitter event today. Mayor David Dinkins and other leading elected officials won't even join the march along Fifth Avenue, and for good reason: by banning a gay and lesbian organization, the parade sponsors are engaging in hateful discrimination. Those who march with them will, whether they mean to or not, appear supportive of their bias."

Who would have thought the *Times* would feel so strongly that they would call, in effect, for the end of the parade? The old Gray Lady ain't what she used to be. I didn't feel that I would be supporting "hateful discrimination" by marching. Nor, I'm sure, did my fellow marchers, many of whom have fought for human rights for years.

I am proud that, as mayor, I issued the first executive order prohibiting discrimination based on sexual orientation in government employment and housing. I was also responsible for introducing and signing into law similar legislation applying to the private sector. When I was mayor, I marched in the Gay Pride parade, and was proud to do so, even though I was vilified by homophobes.

The Ancient Order of Hibernians, the sponsors of the St. Patrick's Day parade, now in its 231st year, has never prohibited gays and lesbians from marching. Gays and lesbians have marched for years without identifying banners. No one asked them about their sex lives—or even their religion—before they marched. The committee has the right to not allow advocacy groups to march as separate contingents, and to forbid advocacy banners and slogans.

This policy applies across the board. If a group of Catholics wanted to march as a separate anti-abortion contingent in the parade, they would not be allowed to, despite the fact that Cardinal O'Connor and the Catholic Church passionately support their cause.

Throughout this debate we have heard the various arguments. A few bear repeating. Would the *Times* support the Ku Klux Klan if it wanted to march in the Martin Luther King Jr. Day parade? Or should right-to-lifers be allowed to march in a pro-choice parade with their banners held high?

To its credit, the Irish Lesbian and Gay Organization (ILGO) conducted itself admirably. Without resorting to violence or civil disobedience, but rather by using the legal process available and being bound by it, they have raised the public consciousness on the issue of discrimination based on sexual orientation.

The Hibernians should be equally commended for fighting to protect their traditions and their constitutional right to freedom of association, and for having used that same legal process.

I marched in the parade and was greeted warmly by many, including the cardinal. But I was booed by the ILGO pickets who shouted, "Shame! Shame!" It was a fine example of "What have you done for me lately?" I doubt that many of them are aware of the origin of the executive order and law which protects their rights—nor do they care. They don't remember that when I was a congressman and they were denied a Parks Department permit to hold the first Gay Pride parade, I went with them and demanded the permit be issued, or a lawsuit would be filed. And, as mayor, I issued the permit that now allows the parade to take place on Fifth Avenue.

I do not criticize Mayor Dinkins for staying away, since he did so as a matter of conscience. However, I suspect that many other public officials made political judgments. They probably read the *Times* editorial and concluded that if they marched, they would lose their liberal credentials.

Politicians who seek public favor by riding the coat-tails of the Irish on joyful occasions should not desert them at the first whiff of controversy. Those who count the house before they cheer or boo are "friends" the Irish community can well do without.

(3/20/92)

Henry Siegman
and the American Jewish Congress

Who would have believed that a dispute between two sophisticated New Yorkers—Alan Dershowitz, a Harvard law professor, and Henry Siegman, executive director of the American Jewish Congress—could end up before a Beit Din, the 4,000-year-old religious court described in the Bible?

The Beit Din was specifically created to settle disputes between Jews.

Siegman has called on the court because he feels he was libeled by Dershowitz in his new bestseller *Chutzpah*.

In the book, Dershowitz recounts how he tried to bring a lawsuit against Jozef Cardinal Glemp, primate of Poland, for defaming Rabbi Avi Weiss. Rabbi Weiss and a group of his followers had gone to Poland in 1989 to protest the continuing presence of a convent at Auschwitz that the Catholic Church had previously agreed to move.

Cardinal Glemp later falsely—and absurdly—accused Rabbi Weiss and his followers of physically threatening the nuns at the convent. In a homily at the Our Lady of Czestochowa shrine, Glemp said, "Recently, a squad of seven Jews from New York launched attacks on the convent at Oswiecim [Auschwitz]." He went on to say, ". . . It did not happen that the sisters were killed or the convent destroyed, because they [the Jews] were apprehended."

After a defamation suit was filed on Rabbi Weiss's behalf, a Polish senator and Dershowitz worked out a statement of retraction with Cardinal Glemp "that would be acceptable to the parties involved in the suit."

But on the day it was to be signed, Henry Siegman and Robert Lifton, president of the American Jewish Congress, met with Cardinal Glemp and allegedly criticized Rabbi Weiss for "contributing to anti-Semitism in Poland." According to Dershowitz, they implied that the Jewish community did not want or need a retraction from the cardinal.

Siegman has called for the Beit Din because he disputes Dershowitz's account. Knowing Henry Siegman, the idea of his invoking such an ancient Orthodox practice can be likened only to Dracula asking for the cross.

Siegman, like many of the executive directors of American Jewish groups, does not represent the current thinking of his constituency. His philosophy is caught in the time warp of the fifties and sixties, when many Jews were afflicted with "Jewish guilt," not because of their own actions but because of those of society in general. They were so anguished by discrimination, especially against blacks, that they believed Jews should make special sacrifices. They went as far as to accept the idea of quotas and preferential treatment, closing their eyes to practices that had long been used as weapons of discrimination against Jews.

I believe Jews should carry out the biblical admonition, "Justice, justice shall thou follow, sayeth the Lord," which, by repeating the word justice, calls for universal justice, not just justice for Jews.

But some Jews, like Henry Siegman, fail to see that while Jews want universal justice, they also want their leaders to make certain they are accorded that same justice. They want them to defend Jews, like Rabbi Avi Weiss, who are not in the mold of the sophisticated, culturally assimilated Jew.

In 1964, I went to the South during "Freedom Summer" to defend blacks who had been deprived of their civil rights. But I did not go out of a sense of guilt. My great-grandfather did not own any slaves. He was himself a slave in Poland, as was my grandfather and father, until the latter two escaped to the United States. I went because it was the right thing to do.

The Jews whom I know want equality before the law for all, not preferential treatment for themselves or others. I believe that many executive directors of Jewish organizations have served too long in their current positions. They are more concerned with their own political agendas, rather than with representing their constituencies.

So it is particularly amusing for me to see Henry Siegman calling on a Beit Din, seeking justice not from his contemporary world, but from the Orthodox Jewish world—moving to the world of the "tallis" from his radical Upper West Side theology.

(7/26/91)

Arlen Specter and Anita Hill

Poor Arlen Specter, the incumbent Republican senator from Pennsylvania who's up for re-election this November. Gloria Steinem and company have decided they will ride to victory on his posterior.

What did he do to deserve this attack? He has been an unflinching defender of women's rights, is a leading supporter of the security of Israel, and is the major liberal voice in the Republican senatorial cadre.

Last fall during the Clarence Thomas confirmation hearings, Specter—doing his job and doing it well—cross-examined Prof. Anita Hill, seeking to ascertain whether she was bearing false witness against Supreme Court nominee Clarence Thomas. He did a superb lawyer's job in questioning Hill's story and successfully impeaching her credibility to the satisfaction of much of America, including up to three-quarters of American women who, when polled, said they did not believe Hill's charges.

What should Specter have done? Treated Hill differently than any other witness because of her gender and race? When Specter successfully led the fight against Reagan nominee Robert Bork, Specter was the darling of the National Organization for Women. As one wag suggested, maybe NOW should change its name to NOW & THEN.

At a recent feminist conference, where Anita Hill as the guest speaker, Gloria Steinem said, "I have a dream [shades of Martin Luther King] that someday we will have in the White House Eleanor Holmes Norton and that she will appoint Anita Hill to the U.S. Supreme Court."

Isn't this the same Eleanor Holmes Norton who, with her husband (both of them lawyers), didn't file District of Columbia income-tax returns for most of the seventies and contended that she was ridiculed for it because she was black? That was her obscene response to tax dodging.

(5/22/92)

The (Former) Soviet Union

The single greatest event in 1991 was the dissolution of the "evil empire," the U.S.S.R.

Two personalities tower over all others in this political drama: Ronald Reagan and Mikhail Gorbachev. Even if you disagreed with Reagan's domestic policies (as I did), he was on target in his handling of the Soviet Union.

Not long ago, when I visited President Reagan in California, he told me that when he and Gorbachev met in 1986 in Reykjavik, Iceland, he took the Soviet leader aside. With only interpreters present, Reagan told Gorbachev: "Mr. President, I want you to know that we will spend whatever it takes to make certain that you are never superior to us militarily." Reagan said he saw Gorbachev gasp and he knew that Gorbachev understood that it was futile to try to gain military superiority over the United States. It was Reagan's inner strength and single-minded sense of purpose that caused Gorbachev to throw in the towel.

Mikhail Gorbachev, like King Lear, created his own Greek tragedy. Like Sadat, Gorbachev is an international martyr, rejected in his own country. He knew the U.S.S.R. could not provide both guns and butter to its people, so he opted for butter. But his move toward democracy and a market economy did not advance with the speed necessary to meet the enhanced expectations of a long-suffering people.

How sad that such an extraordinary, seminal force as Gorbachev should be kicked out of office by midgets. I distrust Boris Yeltsin, who now carries the "black bag" of Armageddon. I fear Yeltsin will turn out to be Russian's equivalent of a "redneck."

The United States is now seeking to create a new economic community with Canada and Mexico to rival the two giants, the European Economic Community and Japan. Wouldn't it make sense for us to organize an even larger common market by offering to bring not only Canada and Mexico into our own economic community, but also the former Soviet republics?

United Germany is now the colossus which bestrides the world stage with the potential—I believe near-certainty—to dominate all of its European common-market partners militarily, economically and in population. If we don't bring the Commonwealth of Independent States into an economic union with us, Germany will reap the benefits. Is it too far-fetched to speculate that Hitler's Third Reich could become Kohl's Fourth Reich, with Russia, et al., willingly included? This time it will be economics, not Stukas, that win the day.

Germany's recent recognition of Slovenia and Croatia against the wishes of its E.E.C. allies is a dangerous harbinger. Slovenia and Croatia were once close allies of Nazi Germany. Slovenia became part of the Third Reich while Croatia became a puppet fascist republic whose Ustashe legions murdered hundreds of thousands of Serbs and tens of thousands of Jews and Gypsies in World War II.

We should not forget that in the early 1920s, long before the Hitler-Stalin pact, the Russians and Germans, then both pariahs, joined forces. Under the Versailles Treaty, the Germans were limited to an army of 100,000 with a small officer corps. The Russians agreed to allow additional German officers to train in Russia. In exchange, Russian soldiers were trained in Germany.

The old Soviet Union was equal to us in space technology and a close second militarily, and it could be again. Far better that the former Soviets retain their current democratic aspirations than turn to an autocratic expansive German Goliath willing and able to finance them in pursuit of a "Pax Germanica."

We should help the former Soviet republics upgrade their economy and become equal partners in a new economic alliance. After all, we are willing to welcome Mexico into an economic alliance and the Mexican economy is replete with problems. Further, Mexico is no threat to us now or in the future. The former Soviet Union could once again become such a threat if we leave it to suffer famine and disgrace.

Remember, there's even a land bridge between us and Russia: It is called Alaska.

(1/3/92)

Spike Lee's Paranoia

I recently saw an interview with Spike Lee, the filmmaker, by ABC-TV's Chris Wallace. Here's the heart of the exchange:

WALLACE: Do the studios care what the message is, or do they just care how much money it makes?

LEE: It depends what the message is. Now, if I did some anti-Semitic thing, like . . .

WALLACE: That wouldn't go down in Hollywood?

LEE: Not at all.

WALLACE: Why not?

LEE: Because a large part of the people that run Hollywood are Jewish. I mean, that's a basic fact.

WALLACE: So is that wrong for them to object to having an anti-Semitic movie:

LEE: No, it's not wrong for them to object. I mean if it's your business, you can do what you want. And when black people start owning our own businesses, running our schools, making our own movies, then we can do what the hell we want to do.

The obvious question for Chris Wallace to have asked was, "Well, when you start making your own movies financed by black bankers so that you can do what you want to do, do you want to make anti-Semitic movies?"

We know his answer. According to *New York Post* film critic David Edelstein, in his new movie *Mo' Better Blues* "Lee makes the Jewish [jazz] club owners Transylvanian ghouls, drooling over black-generated profits as over a batch of necks." The *Village Voice* reviewer, Gary Giddins, says that this part of the movie "undoubtedly is anti-Semitic." The Anti-Defamation League says it is "offensive and stereotypically anti-Semitic."

I haven't seen the movie, but I think we can depend on these critics for a realistic judgment on this issue.

Can you imagine a similar interview with a white director? Say, for example, that Francis Ford Coppola said on national TV that he'd like to do an anti-black movie. Does anyone think he'd get any money to do films of any kind, from white, black and especially Jewish bankers? What would the NAACP be saying?

Banks don't finance anti-Semitic or anti-black movies because of moral conscience and because—more importantly—such movies wouldn't be profitable. They would be rejected by a great majority of people in this country, and denounced by every reviewer and every editorial writer.

Why am I so concerned about Spike Lee? His comments are part of a larger picture. In July, the NAACP invited Legrand Clegg, who according to the ADL has a history of anti-Semitism, to speak at a workshop. At the workshop, Mr. Clegg charged that there was collective "Jewish racism" and excessive Jewish influence in Hollywood. According to the *Los Angeles Times*, he engaged in "familiar anti-Semitic calumnies and con-spirational innuendos."

You would think that Ben Hooks, executive director of the NAACP, would apologize for having invited this well-known anti-Semite to participate, and repudiate his racist views. Instead, Mr. Hooks said, "We have 29 workshops with 125 pan-elists and we do not take responsibility for their statements. We neither agree nor disagree with what they say . . . We don't have a position because we haven't done a study on it, but we do know there is racism in Hollywood."

As for Mr. Clegg's comments, Ben Hook said, "We do not agree with the statement but we do not exercise thought con-trol. I would not invite a panelist here and then say you cannot say this or that."

The allegation by Spike Lee and Legrand Clegg that Holly-wood is "owned" by Jews is intended to encourage anti-Semi-tism. But let's assume that the Jews who helped start the film industry seventy-five years ago continue to play a large role in acting, directing, producing and financing. Do they have to apologize for that? Is it possible it occurs because of individual talent and investment opportunities?

In that light, I wrote to Ben Hooks: "There is a danger in all of this that you, and others like you, are causing others like myself to conclude that supporting the NAACP and its objectives is becoming a one-way street."

I have yet to hear from him.

(8/10/90)

Taxes

What causes me to believe that half of this town is off the books? Personal experience.

Now that I am in the private sector, I need someone to clean my house on a daily basis, so I've been looking around to find and hire a housekeeper.

I thought I was offering a reasonable wage ($10 per hour). Many expressed interest in the position. But that changed when I told the applicants they would have to pay income taxes on their salary, I would have to pay income taxes on their salary, I would have to file a Social Security report, and we would both have to pay the FICA tax. The response? "If you want me, it has to be off the books."

Now, I couldn't do that. I've never knowingly violated any tax laws. I released my income-tax returns every year as congressman and as mayor. And while I don't have to do that now that I've left public life, I still intend to pay my taxes in full, and to give the government the benefit of every doubt.

I remember well the anxiety I felt as mayor when my accountant first told me I was being audited. He told me, "Don't worry, everything's OK." I worried anyway.

The outcome? I had overpaid by $450 (my accountant had prepared the return), which the government was returning to me. My accountant (nice guy) only charged $750 to represent me in that audit.

Consider this example of how taxes go uncollected. According to a report by *Daily News* columnist Mike McAlary, labor leader Victor Gotbaum and his wife, Betsy—recently appointed parks commissioner by Mayor Dinkins—were vacationing in 1984 in a villa in Mexico, where they become friendly with the maid, a woman named Isabel Garcia.

Six months later, Ms. Garcia and her son came to the U.S. for medical treatment. She remained here—apparently as an illegal alien—and worked for the Gotbaums for the last five years, in violation of the law.

The Gotbaums paid her $100 a week in what they refer to as expense money. They say they paid the rest of her $15,000 annual salary into an escrow account held in their name. They did this, says Victor Gotbaum, on the advice of counsel. The bank book, it should be noted, has not been made available.

This sounds like peonage to me. In any event, it represents highly peculiar behavior for a major labor-union leader ostensibly concerned with protecting domestic jobs. But it's the question of paying taxes that I'm raising.

Change the names of Victor and Betsy Gotbaum to Harry and Leona Helmsley, and ask what action should be taken.

The Gotbaums appear to have violated the immigration laws of this country; then—it would seem—they failed to pay someone adequately for her labor. And they are responsible for the government not having collected income and Social Security taxes.

Would this have been a one-day, one-reporter story if it concerned the Helmsleys?

(2/9/90)

The *New York Times*

There once was a newspaper that had a problem. It was accused by some of its employees of discrimination. The editors and managers believed they were innocent. What to do?

The newspaper was the the *New York Times* and when it was confronted with a lawsuit that it knew could mean picket lines, boycotts and an embarrassing judgment costing it money damages, the *Times* chose to settle. In this case, to twist the words of Shakespeare, "settling was the better part of valor."

And then, apparently deciding that this agreement did not fit under the rubric "All the News That's Fit to Print," the *Times* insisted that the court seal the file. So much for the public's right to know. However, it was common knowledge that one aspect of the agreement called for preferential hiring, assignment and promotion of minorities.

Given this past unfortunate experience, no organization should be more aware than the *Times* of the dangers inherent in any law that might encourage quotas. And yet, on April 7, they published an editorial on the pending Civil Rights Act (HR1) that is as "politically correct" as one can get. One wonders what has happened to their highly regarded fair and intelligent editorial judgment.

The editorial begins, "There's probably no more incendiary epithet in presence discourse than the word 'quota.' " It goes on to say, "but calling something a quota does not make it one." The fact is that opponents of HR1, myself included, do not refer to HR1 as explicitly requiring quotas, but allege that it will inevitably result in the widespread adoption of quotas. And it will.

How? Because HR1 presumes that every employment force should reflect the demographics of the available work force on the basis of race, nationality, religion and gender. If statistically it doesn't at every job title, there is a presumption of employer discrimination, difficult to overcome, and the potential of large backpay awards.

Another issue emerging from this debate, addressed in an editorial by the *Wall Street Journal*, is "race norming," is an employment practice that adjusts job-test scores according to separate racial percentiles.

This means that whites, blacks and Hispanics are ranked by percentile against only members of their race. When an employer gets these results, they have been merged together without reference to race and listed by rank. Thus, someone whose actual score on a the test was high could be listed at a lower percentile than someone whose actual score was lower, but whose percentile-within-race was higher. Is this the American dream of equality?

The *Times* editorial goes on to say that "for eighteen years before the Supreme Court changed the rule, 'business necessity' was defined in the fuller way—and there was no employer rush to quotas."

I would not concede that point. There has been testimony in Congress that some employers quietly resort to quotas to avoid lawsuits. Moreover, the Civil Rights Bill of 1990, as well as the current bill, go well beyond the law established in the case of *Griggs* v. *Duke Power*. In a *Times* story of October 26, Morton Halperin of the American Civil Liberties Union, a supporter of the legislation, said, "We thought that, given the current Supreme Court and its demonstrated hostility toward civil rights, the language had to be stronger to get the result we think Griggs mandated."

Even the alternative legislation proposed by the Bush administration goes too far. It retains the HR1 provision which forces the employer to prove his innocence. This flies in the face of American jurisprudence—innocent until proven guilty.

If a large and powerful operation like the *New York Times* felt it had to settle instead of contesting discrimination charges which it believed to be untrue, what would a small businessman do under the weight of harsher legislation which would give employees even more leverage to press an accusation of discrimination.

The majority of people in our society are fundamentally decent and desirous of doing that which is right, but they will not tolerate, in the case of equality, making their children second-class citizens. End discrimination, but not with measures that lead to reverse discrimination.

(4/12/91)

Unions

As I said early this year in this column: New York City is a basket case. Why?

For starters, Mayor Dinkins thought he and the municipal union leaders were partners in government. Wrong!

As mayor, David Dinkins is responsible for the welfare of 7½ million residents. The union leaders have a different agenda: more pay for less work with higher pensions.

When I was elected mayor in 1977, I met with major municipal union leaders. They were very friendly, even though they had supported Mario Cuomo, not me, in the primary. During the meeting, their consultant, Jack Bigel, said to me that we—the city and the unions—were partners.

I said to him, "You represent 300,000 people. I represent 7½ million, of which your 300,000 are a part. And it is terrific when we are all on the same track. But sometimes we are not going to be. So we are not partners. And everybody should know that."

When David Dinkins was elected, the unions believed the mayor owed them—and, apparently, he believed it as well. After all, he had won the general election by less than 2 percent. When the labor contracts came up, the unions demanded unaffordable pay increases. And Mayor Dinkins agreed to give the teachers a 5.8 percent raise, which set the pattern for other municipal unions. Meanwhile, in the private sector, tens of thousands were being laid off and the economy was in a recession.

Like Scarlett O'Hara, the mayor preferred to think about the city's financial problems tomorrow. While he is not responsible for the recession, he has compounded the problem by not imposing a hiring and wage freeze early on.

With the city teetering at the precipice, he finally asked his "partners" for givebacks. They have responded with Bronx jeers. There is a greater likelihood of the Messiah appearing tomorrow than Barry Feinstein of the Teamsters, Sandy Feldman of the UFT and Stanley Hill of DC 37 agreeing to anything but sham givebacks.

(4/26/91)

Vampires

A recent caller to my WABC radio show reported that he has observed large numbers of human vampires walking the streets of New York City. Did I, he asked, have a remedy for dealing with this problem? I told him that upon meeting a vampire, he should immediately display his crucifix or mezuza. Then he should follow the vampire back to his or her crypt and drive a stake through its heart as it lies in its coffin. My caller thanked me profusely, as you will should you meet a vampire. My secretary asked, "Was he serious?" I told her, "I don't know, but I am."

(6/19/92)

Cyrus Vance

Cyrus Vance is the Neville Chamberlain of our time. With the best of intentions, he made Serbian bestiality possible. He, therefore, shares responsibility for the assassination of the deputy prime minister of Bosnia, the rapes of 20,000 Muslim women, and the suffering of tens of thousands of civilians in Sarajevo. Why? Because he successfully urged the U.S. arms embargo against Bosnia, opposed military efforts to free Sarajevo, and is now rewarding Serbian aggression by divvying up Bosnia. Remember the Sudetenland?

The *New York Times* editorial board, along with *Times* columnists Anthony Lewis and Leslie Gelb, cannot bring themselves to harshly criticize Vance. Could it be because Vance is a member of the *Times*'s board of directors?

(1/22/93)

Sol Wachler

Why did 250 state judges give a standing ovation at Tavern on the Green to former Chief Justice Sol Wachler, who is awaiting sentencing for his crimes? Commiseration, sympathy and handshakes from old friends were in order, but applause for a man who terrorized his former lover and her daughter?

Robert Wagner

Bob Wagner was a prince of the city. If we were living in the days of ancient Greece, the Kingdoms of Israel and Judah or the city-state of Troy, the citizenry would be rending their garments, wailing to the heavens and carrying his body through the streets on his shield.

Bobby, as everyone who knew him called him, always knew he was royalty. Royal by right of the contributions made by his grandfather, that great visionary senator. Royal because of the achievements of his father, that great three-term mayor, who always will be remembered with the same reverence as Fiorello LaGuardia. Royal because he continued the family tradition of public service as chairman of the City Planning Commission, deputy mayor and president of the Board of Education.

As we have seen this week from the comments of those who knew Bobby well, he was considered one of those special people who appear among us for a short time, lighting our way with their unique genius. While they are not perfect, their shining intellects soar as we see them perform, and then come to a final rest.

Bobby's career in public life took a great toll on him. He was constantly called upon to solve problems that others found daunting. Genius is not submissive to time clocks and appointment schedules; Bobby often led his friends to the point of despair, if not anger, when he would be very late to an appointment or, worse, not keep it without calling to cancel.

But nobody stayed angry for long. Exasperated, yes. Angry, no. We recognized we were working with a man who was vulnerable and entitled to his frailties. Who could stay angry with this young man whose Irish smile — or was it Scottish or German — always beguiled the observer? He often was viewed as a man/child: In intellect among the greatest in our city, yet retaining the curiosity of a child.

Bobby was more respectful of the rights of other people than anyone I've ever met. He would be as courteous to a street vagrant as he would be to the cardinal, and I've seen him in conversations with both. To him, listening was more important than talking. But when he spoke, he made not only common sense, he overwhelmed you with his intelligence and compassion.

There are not very many visionaries in this world who can plan out 10, 20, 50 years for the city. President George Bush spoke of the "vision thing." Bobby had it, and brought it to a higher plane than anyone I've ever met.

He never sought perks for himself. When he was entitled to the use of a personal car as part of his city obligations, he declined the opportunity. Instead, he would usually take the subway to display confidence in the system. Without bombast or fanfare, he endorsed Rudy Giuliani. In doing, so he irritated his partner, pollster Lou Harris, who, Bobby told me, suspended him from the partnership until after the election and directed him not to enter the premises.

But Bobby never regretted his endorsement, even though it also irritated his close friends Richard Wade and Arthur

Schlesinger Jr., the latter to a lesser extent. Bobby told me he was upbraided by them for his failure to adopt the expected position of Democratic Party loyalty. He made the endorsement because he believed Giuliani's election to be in the best interests of the city. His endorsement and commercial turned out to be the most significant contributions anyone made to Giuliani's election. People had trust in the name Wagner: New York's noble family.

Following Giuliani's victory, Bobby told me how important it was for the new mayor and his wife, Donna, to protect their children from being overwhelmed by the attention they would receive in their day-to-day lives. He recalled his years living in Gracie Mansion in the late '50's and early '60's, and said those years could either build a child's character or destroy it. We know it built his, and he wanted to be sure the Giulianis were aware of the pitfalls that lay in wait.

Finally, Bobby, the sophisticated man, participant in all the changes of the 20th century, never lost his faith in his religion, Roman Catholicism. He attended Mass regularly at St. Joseph's Church in his Yorkville neighborhood. He did not wear a hair shirt or lecture others, but tried to live his life in accordance with Catholic principles, always ready to face God when God would call him. For those of us who loved him, he has been prematurely called. I know he met his maker unafraid.

Goodbye, gentle prince: Day is done, the night reigns.

(11/19/93)

Andrew Young

Despite Andy Young's debacle at the United Nations in the late 1970s, his involvement in the BCCI scandal is still shocking. When I was in Congress, he was the most respected member, a man of intelligence, courage and integrity, minister and confidant of Martin Luther King. But later, as U.S. ambassador to the United Nations, he fell from grace for holding secret meetings with the PLO in violation of State Department regulations. He resigned under fire.

Young has now admitted that last year BCCI forgave a $150,000 loan to his consulting firm. This would not make headlines except that BCCI is no ordinary bank. It's an Arab scam whose depositers include organized-crime figures, terrorists, gun runners and drug dealers. Young joins two other Georgians who received benefits from BCCI—former President Carter and Bert Lance, Carter's former budget director. Carter received $8 million for his charities and Lance sold his bank to BCCI, a transaction that is now under investigation. Now we know why these three were hostile to Israel.

(9/7/91)

FOUR

Ed Koch Goes to the Movies

The Age of Innocence (−)

I'm sorry folks—this movie is a big bore.

When I asked those leaving as I waited to enter, a dozen people, recognizing me, separately came over and said, in one form or other, the equivalent of "a wonderful movie." Only one woman said, "It's a little slow." I now know she wasn't telling the whole truth; it's a lot slow.

The others may have liked the movie because of its tableaus, the sheer beauty of the scenes, or its attention to detail; or perhaps they liked Michelle Pfeiffer or Daniel Day-Lewis, and any or all of those aspects were enough for them. But not for me. A movie has to involve me, grip me, best of all enthrall me if I am to consider it worthy of a plus and recommending it. Obviously this movie did not.

A movie made fifty years ago by Orson Welles, *The Magnificent Ambersons*, covers roughly the same Victorian age and does it with excitement. It's available on videos. Check it out.

Alien 3 (–)

Alien 3 is a schlock film capitalizing on the earlier two, which I think I remember as being good; I'm not sure anymore. This film has very little plot, minimalist acting and tries to pass off people constantly running up and down tunnels as action.

The alien resembles a Tyrannosaurus Rex but, frankly, this one wouldn't scare a Brontosaurus: It didn't scare me. It doesn't run, it scurries. It reminded me of a mouse I recently saw scurrying across a kitchen floor. Don't ask whose kitchen. That mouse created more terror than the alien.

I read that they had to induce Sigourney Weaver to do this film. I can understand why. They must have paid her big bucks. The primates of *Gorillas in the Mist* were better actors than most of Sigourney's fellow perpetrators, and I must, in all candor, say that Sigourney didn't help much either. If all they wanted was a woman with a shaved head, they could have asked Sinead O'Connor. I don't like Sinead O'Connor's politics or her singing, but I admire her pluck and her genuine odd-ball looks. I cannot say the same for Sigourney Weaver.

The problem is that we are now accustomed to hundred million dollar sci-fi movies with special effects, e.g. *Terminator II*, that boggle your mind, so when a movie doesn't have them you are reminded of the sci-fi serials of the '30s and '40s, which entertained those of us who can recall that age, and which lacked the sophistication that we all now pretend to or actually have. Then movies cost a dime and for that you got two movies, one serial, a Coke and a comic book—so special effects were not on our minds. When you contrast that with the $7.50 you pay today when you get only a stinker like this, you will understand my outrage at those who put this garbage on the screen. This movie is making lots of money and is number three or four in the country in box office grosses. I am losing faith in my fellow moviegoers, but I promise you I will never ride with the lowest common denominator.

We are left with the impression that both Sigourney and the alien die. Don't believe it. They'll be back. There is too much money to be made in repeating this travesty.

American Heart (−)

Sadly, I must report that this movie is another manifestation of studio hype aided and abetted by reviewers. Everywhere you look lately, on television and in the papers, there's another interview with the movie's star, Jeff Bridges. We are told that he is one of the most underrated actors in Hollywood and that, finally, his time has come. This movie, the interviewers convey, will reveal his artistry for all to see. Not to me.

When I decided to see this movie, I was prepared for an art film. You know, a small film, delicate, beautifully crafted, insightful, uplifting, a breakthrough, one that allows the audience to feel its emotions and care about the characters without resorting to soap opera. *American Heart* may very well qualify as an art film, which means it will appeal to a limited audience: masochists.

A huge problem in the movie is the sound track. Maybe it was the theater I saw it in, but about a third of the sound track was inaudible, so I was constantly straining to hear.

It is a one-note picture. Jack (Bridge's character) is part of the underclass, but there are no major variations in his lifestyle, no revelations about how his squalid life is affecting him: no surprises.

American Me (+)

I went to see this film with great anticipation and I was not disappointed. Having seen the half dozen serious films by black directors and/or writers released over the last year depicting the rage of the black underclass, I wanted to see how a Mexican-American director dealt with similar circumstances in the Hispanic community.

American Me opens with a depiction of what became known as the "zoot suit" riots in the 1940s. I dimly recall the riots themselves, but I vividly remember the serious and well-received play *Zoot Suit* which the director and star of *American Me*, Edward James Olmos, starred in on Broadway. The energy he displays on stage manifests itself once again in this film. He is a fine director and actor; he received an Oscar nomination for *Stand and Deliver* a few years ago.

I saw the film on a Friday night and was surprised that the theater was only half full. The audience was reflective of the gorgeous mosaic: an equal division of Hispanics, blacks and whites. Regrettably a handful of patrons yelled out obscenities at different moments and laughed inappropriately at particularly brutal scenes. I thought to myself, "Gee, I'd like to yell out, 'Shut up you jerk'" but discretion prevailed. But what a shame that the management didn't attempt to control the hecklers. Of course, how can you expect some young usher, male or female, to handle a situation like that? So we all bore it stoically while harboring thoughts of murder, similar to those acted out on the screen. If thoughts were subject to criminal prosecution, we all would have been arrested.

Basic Instinct (+)

This movie is a traditional "whodunit" with lots of explicit sex and even more blood and gore than usual. Both principals, Sharon Stone and Michael Douglas, appear frequently in the nude not only in their coupling, but simply when walking around.

Michael Douglas's nudity is carefully choreographed so as to avoid frontal views, although his rear is often displayed. When he and Stone are in bed, you see a lot of her, while he is art-fully draped either by the bed linens or her body.

Gay groups have said this film is homophobic because Sharon Stone plays a bisexual and she and her live-in-lesbian lover (Leilani Sarelle) are portrayed as evil. They are suspects in a murder investigation being conducted by police detective Douglas, with whom Stone is also involved. Ridiculous. Most films involving crime triangles traditionally have a heterosexual threesome. Does the heterosexuality of the suspects in those films make them examples of "heterophobia"?

I agree with those who say there should be more films depicting gays and lesbians sympathetically by allowing them the same range of character and personality as heterosexuals. There has been a rise in bias crimes against homosexuals and Hollywood should take the lead in helping educate the public, as it did in the 1960s when more sympathetic films with stronger black roles emerged from Hollywood. Such efforts might help reduce homophobia.

There were no pickets at the theater when I attended. The house was full. This movie will make a lot of money for Douglas and will propel Stone to stardom.

Billy Bathgate (−)

Billy Bathgate is an absolute bomb. I am a devotee of Dustin Hoffman and his acting is normally brilliant. None of his performances will ever match *The Graduate*, but *Rain Man* and *Tootsie* sure came close. In every one of those films he created a real person.

In *Billy Bathgate* he plays Dutch Schultz, but he never brings Schultz to life. Everything about him seems false including his voice.

If I weren't reviewing this movie, I would have walked out. But reviewers, at least this reviewer, feel an obligation to stay until the bitter end.

large numbers of young men to prison. We need to reinstate the draft, this time as a civilian service corps for young people to serve in for two years beginning at the age of eighteen. The young men and women who are disaffiliated and become part of the criminal corps in our inner cities will only be saved in large numbers if they are physically taken out of this environment.

This is a chilling movie with a sociological sock that will give you great pause. Where is our nation headed?

Chain of Desire (+)

There are fourteen characters in this movie. Each is seen separately acting out their sexual fantasies. The fantasies include fetishism, bondage, heterosexual coupling, homosexual coupling, bisexual coupling, autoerotism, masturbation and voyeurism. There are several obvious omissions, including S and M and lesbianism: A quibble considering there is so much else on your plate.

There are no scenes of frontal nudity, female or male, except breasts. But remember, the New York Court of Appeals said women can appear bare breasted any place in this city at any time. And they do. There was one in Washington Square Park the other day. A cop asked her to put her shirt on. She said, "Get lost. I know my rights." He left and proceeded to give a summons to a boom box carrier.

This movie is a sizzler just like the ads say. It is never crude, often poignant and you can choose your aberration or stay mainstream. Clearly, "Chacun a son gout." I believe it is fair to label this film as soft porn, but it is being shown in mainstream moviehouses.

The closing scene takes place in the nightclub where the film opened. Almost all of the lovers are there dancing the night away. AIDS is mentioned indirectly when Alma is told on the phone by her former lover that he is sick and going home to his family. He tells her to "get tested."

Before the credits, there is a panoramic helicopter night view of the beautiful towers of Manhattan among which are the Empire State Building, Chrysler Building, the Citicorp Center and much more. This scene alone makes the film worth seeing.

Chaplin (+)

This could have been a great picture; it was not. However, it is worth seeing, if only for the last ten minutes of this two-and-a-half-hour film. Those closing minutes contain brief excerpts of Chaplin's early films: *The Tramp*, *The Gold Rush*, *City Lights*, *Limelight* (with its haunting score), *The Great Dictator*, and *Modern Times*. Tears ran down my cheeks as I watched those brief vignettes. Why? The poignancy, brilliance of intellect and the humor displayed were simply overwhelming. We have had nothing equal to Chaplin's talent since his death in 1977.

The script is based on Chaplin's *My Autobiography* and a biography written by David Robinson entitled *Chaplin: His Life and Art*. I have read neither, but I'm certain they are better than the movie which used them. Why? The movie simply did not achieve its goal of showing the many facets of Chaplin, the genius, which we intuitively know he had because of the extraordinary movies he made and amazing life he led.

Chaplin's sexual proclivities, including his many liaisons and marriages, and his final marriage to Oona O'Neill, who bore him eight children, are depicted in some detail but inadequately.

The references to Chaplin's political involvement and scenes of J. Edgar Hoover harassing him, which ultimately led to Chaplin's being "exiled" in Europe for over twenty years, are portrayed without passion, indeed, woodenly. Robert Downey Jr.'s performance as the young Charlie Chaplin doing the Tramp and his real life are well done—indeed a tour de force.

But the same cannot be said of Downey's characterization of Chaplin as an old man who at the opening of the movie is discussing his autobiography with his editor George Hayden (Anthony Hopkins). Again in the ending crawl we learn the editor was a fictional character used as a device to introduce the flashbacks and propel the movie forward. The technique did not enhance the movie although Hopkins performed his part well.

Cliffhanger (−)

The French have a word for this movie—*merde*! It cost a fortune—some reports say as much as $75 million—because of the special effects related to mountain climbing. Undoubtedly, the location shoot (it was filmed in the Italian Alps, but is portrayed as taking place in the Rockies) must have taken its toll on the budget and the comfort of the actors. Too bad the effort and expense weren't worth it. None of the principal actors performed well—maybe they were too cold.

Convicts (−)

Those who created *Convicts* should be punished. Having recently enjoyed Robert Duvall and Lukas Haas in *Rambling Rose*—which was simply a delight—I looked forward to seeing them in what I hoped would be another tour de force. It wasn't.

The story is incredibly weak and it was hard not to fall asleep. I don't think I did, but who can ever be sure? Duvall is the consummate actor, but to give this movie rave reviews based simply on his presence—and many have praised the movie—is nonsense.

Everyone I spoke with at the theater, with one exception, found it boring. The exception said yes it was boring, but so is

Chekhov's *The Cherry Orchard* and everyone enjoys that! Not everyone, thought I.

The Crying Game (+)

This film, by Irish director Neil Jordan, is dramatic, bizarre, exciting, kinky and poignant with exceptional acting.

Everybody performs their part, small or big, exceptionally well, but the only two principals are Stephen Rea and Jaye Davidson, and they are superb. Adrian Dunbar as Maguire, the leader of the IRA gang, and Jim Broadbent as Col, the bartender at the cabaret bar, are perfect in their supporting roles. There are very few films that I've seen that I could call perfect—without a single cavil—but this is one I can say meets that definition.

Damage (+)

The title comes from a line in the film which goes something like "damaged people do great harm." And believe me, the principals in this film, Dr. Stephen Fleming (Jeremy Irons) and Anna Barton (Juliette Binoche) are damaged and do more than great harm—they create a Greek tragedy.

The film is really a case study of two sexually dysfunctional people, right out of Krafft-Ebing. Normally, the reference to dysfunctional in the context of sex refers to people who can't make it together or with others for neurotic reasons. In this Krafft-Ebing analysis we are privy to two people who can make it anywhere: on the floor, on tables, standing up, sitting down, and in the doorway of a building on a public street, fully clothed at high noon.

Last Tango in Paris with Marlon Brando and Maria Schneider introduced heterosexual anal intercourse to the big screen, to be seen by a cross-section audience, free to buy their tickets at the box office and boldly walk in without fear of being seen by neighbors, friends, or colleagues. Watching *Damage*, you may experience a flashback to that sexual romp if you saw it.

But any recollection you may have will pale when compared with the obsession these two lovers have for one another. What is interesting, however, is how devoid this film is of true passion. I doubt there was one viewer in the theater who was sexually aroused by the numerous couplings depicted. Why? They lacked the emotion of love, caring and tenderness that ought to be a part of the sex act if there is to be a sense of gratification.

These almost daily liaisons generally involved violence practiced by Dr. Fleming against Anna; some of the moments surely bordered on rape, even if Anna enjoyed what was happening and was not only a willing participant, but solicited the assault. However, the movie is never raunchy or embarrassing because of the fine acting of its principals.

I don't recall ever having seen Irons in any role other than one that required him to be to some degree debauched. His anorexic physical look lends added realism to his magnificent acting. Each role he has had from *Brideshead* to *Dead Ringers* to *Reversal of Fortune* called for tour de force performances and on each occasion he rose to that level.

Anna's mother, Elizabeth, is played by Leslie Caron. Remember her from *Lili*? She will now remind you of Hermoine Gingold, who was a great actress.

The Distinguished Gentleman (−)

Having served for nine years in Congress, I know that there is a lot to be parodied and satirized, but this movie didn't have the faintest idea how to do it. Watching this film, it was clear that the writers were using a television sitcom as their model, and one with very low standards. I also think the writers had the notion that this was a good opportunity to demonstrate politi-

cal correctness and bash an overwhelmingly white, male insti-
tution. Unfortunately, it was done so heavy-handedly it lost its
wallop.

Eddie Murphy should take a break in his career and go back
to *Saturday Night Live* even for a short stint to get in touch with
himself and his audience. Based on news reports and his recent
movies, he seems to have bought his own act.

Doc Hollywood (+)

The critics have praised *Doc Hollywood*, but also denigrated it by
labeling it "a summer movie." Ridiculous. It is a superb movie
for all seasons.

The picture is a throwback to the comedies of the forties,
updated for the nineties, with slightly more sophisticated language and a little nudity thrown in. It is reminiscent of *State
Fair*, *Oklahoma* and Thornton Wilder's *Our Town*.

Doc Hollywood stars Michael J. Fox as a young doctor fresh
out of medical school. He wants to specialize in plastic surgery
and work in L.A., the lucrative land of the good life and multi-
ple facelifts. On his way to L.A. he ends up, through a series of
plausible, serendipitous acts, in the small town of Grady, South
Carolina. Everyone in this lovely Southern town is not only
charming, but believably so.

The town could be Brigadoon—a mystical, lovely fantasy
with people you care about. It has everything going for it—
except a resident doctor. The townspeople try to get Fox to
change his mind and set up practice in their hamlet.

There is no violence, no blood, no gore, and your interest
never flags. The nudity is tastefully done, so it is a movie that
the whole family can see.

I mean no disrespect but if, as may be the case, Michael J.
Fox is denied some roles in the future because of his size, we
will be the loser. He can do anything. When he is acting on the
screen, he is six feet tall. Remember Alan Ladd? He was proba-

bly shorter than Fox, but it didn't stop him—and his movies were blood and guts.

Again, this is not just a summer movie. Go see it in the fall if it is still playing.

Dogfight (−)

I went to see *Dogfight* wanting to like the film. River Phoenix is a young actor whose name is intriguing and is reported to be on his birth certificate. I had seen and enjoyed his performances in two previous films, *Running on Empty* and *Stand by Me*. I have always thought he was another Brandon De Wilde, who was also magnificent in adolescent roles, but who unfortunately died before achieving cinematic success as an adult. You may remember him from *Shane*.

In this film, Phoenix plays a young man who has just completed marine boot camp and is being sent to Vietnam. Even though this film is set in 1963, I thought it would bring back memories for me of 1943 when I, also age 19, had just come out of army basic training; it did and it didn't. I thought I would be reliving my youth vicariously. Although the young soldiers, with their camaraderie and constant use of obscenities, did remind me in sight and sound of my fellow soldiers in 1943, it still didn't work for me. River Phoenix is not yet Richard Gere. *Dogfight* is not *An Officer and a Gentleman* by any stretch.

It is with regret that I separate myself from Roger Ebert, Rex Reed and Dennis Cunningham, three movie critics who praised the film. Cunningham called it "one of the year's best."

I await River Phoenix's next film and I hope the river runs smoother next time.

El Mariachi (+)

This movie, scripted, directed and produced by Robert Rodriguez, is a gem. It was made for $7,500 by an unknown, using unknown actors and on less than a shoestring, and has vaulted Rodriguez to stardom. For his next movie, he has been given a $6 million budget by a major studio. I saw Rodriguez, who is American, being interviewed on the *Charlie Rose Show* late one evening and was fascinated by his humor and sophistication, notwithstanding the fact that he can be no more than twenty-five years old. He recounts how he had sold a major agent in L.A. on his film by sheer chutzpah, calling him on the phone, convincing him to look at a video of his film.

I went with H.K., both of us thinking that we would see a $7,500 beginner's film which would be a tour de force, but still more or less a homemade video. Instead, we saw a fully entertaining, first-class flick in every way, including acting, script and humor. H.K. said, "This film was wonderful on its own and needs no excuses to defend itself."

The movie has a number of well-done gory shoot-outs, and chase scenes. They are as good as any you've seen in movies costing millions. You also get some mariachi singing (not enough, regrettably) and a surprise ending that would never have happened in a traditional million-dollar version, but which makes absolute sense and fits this movie like a glove.

Farewell My Concubine (+)

This is a very good movie, but not the great movie that some critics are touting it to be. It affects your senses in the same way *The Last Emperor* did, but the story line isn't as compelling.

The enormous time span involved covers the warlord period in China; the government of General Chiang Kai-shek and the Kuomintang; World War II; the barbarism of the Cultural Revolution led by Chairman Mao; and finally the present—a relatively tranquil period notwithstanding the current government's repression of dissidents. It is a canvas that envelops you and shows you aspects of China that few have ever seen.

I found the warlord era especially interesting. It had nothing to do with war or government. Instead, it was the equivalent of the English Dickinsonian era replete with the exploitation of children, Chinese style.

The movie opens with a street scene, and throngs of Chinese buying, walking and watching a group of young boys perhaps 11 to 16 years old performing circus style on the street. We see a young woman walking with a child whose face, when uncovered, is androgynous. She is a prostitute seeking to find a place for her son whom she can no longer keep at the brothel. She tries to give him to the master of an opera academy where boys are trained for performance. A particular opera, *Farewell My Concubine*, is their repertory piece. The master refuses to accept the boy initially because he has a deformity of the hand that, he said, "would scare the audience." The deformity is a sixth finger on one hand. You can guess how that is disposed of.

The boy grows up in the academy, which teaches the boys their craft, overwhelmingly through cruelty. The boys are treated like circus animals of yesterday and beaten into submission. They are beaten if they are bad, and they are beaten if they are good. Why when good? Because, says the master, "Now you'll remember what was good and you'll duplicate it."

The young boy, Dieyi (played as an adult by Leslie Cheung), is raised to perform the role of the concubine in the opera. In response to the question, "Who is he?" he must learn to respond that he is a girl. He refuses time and again, intentionally singing that he is a boy until he is beaten into submission and accepts his role in life, to be a courtesan—a girl.

His friend, a protector among the boys, is Xiaolou (played as an adult by Zhang Fengyi) who grows up to be the actor performing the role of the king in the opera. Early on it's clear that Dieyi is attracted to Xiaolou; it is not clear if those feelings are returned.

There is a poignant, piteous scene in which Dieyi is given for sexual purposes for a night to an old Mandarin official whom we see in bed with a young girl. When Dieyi is brought to his room, the official dismisses the girl child and attacks the boy child who is petrified and runs around the room to escape, but is ultimately caught and dragged to bed.

Dieyi and Xiaolou mature before your eyes. Dieyi develops into a beautiful young man who, by movement, facial expression and dress, is clearly a courtesan. Xiaolou becomes involved with Juxian [Gong Li], a prostitute whom he rescues from a brothel.

The movie records the impact of societal change by showing the way the Chinese opera troupe and the opera itself is received by audiences. The most dramatic and onerous change in the government and the public's view towards the opera takes place during chairman Mao's Cultural Revolution. There we see Dieyi and Xiaolou hooted when on stage and tortured when off. They are forced to confess to political deviancy and betray their friend, and are subjected to crowd catcalls and blows as they are paraded through the streets. The current era, which follows that period in the film, is far more beneficent to them. The opening scene of the film depicts the present; the rest is told in flashbacks in Mandarin with English subtitles.

Having praised the movie, why do I caution and convey that you should not expect the Second Coming? A major reason is the failure to examine more closely the day-to-day relationship between Dieyi and Xiaolou or to adequately explore the relationship between Xiaolou and Juxian. Both should have been given more attention. One powerful scene is the closing denouement when Xialou and Juxian, now husband and wife, having come out of the Cultural Revolution alive, get drunk and go to bed together. Without their knowledge, Dieyi stands on the porch watching what for him is an extremely erotic scene between this woman and this man whom he, at the very least, fantasizes as his lover.

The movie is an outstanding example of the many new Chinese films reaching our screens. They do not yet measure up to the Japanese films that we have become accustomed to, but they will, of that you can be sure.

Fearless (+)

This is a brilliant film. The script creates an extraordinary mood, as does the fine acting of all its principals.

The opening is spectacular. You see a cornfield with people walking single file following a striking-looking long-haired man who is carrying an infant and holding the hand of an adolescent boy. Then you see the ruins of a plane fuselage and realize you have come upon a wrecked plane and are witnessing the immediate aftermath of an enormous tragedy.

Medical personnel are assisting people and carrying them from the scene. Suddenly, one woman, Carla Rodrigo (Rosie Perez) begins screaming and fighting those carrying her. You are overwhelmed by the pain she conveys in her writhing, her face, and her outstretched hands. She wants to run back into the plane to save her infant son left behind who is either dead or will die in an instant as the plane explodes.

Then we meet the survivors: the leader of those walking through the cornfield, Max Klein (Jeff Bridges), and the young boy with him, Byron Hummel (Daniel Cerny). From that point on, flashbacks are interwoven with the present.

The flashbacks show us panic on the plane as the passengers learn of the impending crash. The stewardess, a young woman (Cordis Heard), is terrified but nevertheless does her job helping passengers prepare for the impact. Klein, an architect, who is flying from San Francisco when the disaster occurs on the outskirts of Bakersfield, is sitting with his partner Jeff Gordon (John DeLancie), who seems to be the head of the firm: we later learn he was decapitated in the crash, although we see no blood and guts at any time.

As Klein leads some of the survivors from the plane there is an ethereal quality about him during and following the tragedy. We later learn he is married to Laura (Isabella Rossellini), and has a son, Jonah (Spencer Vrooman), who have to contend with the changes in Max's personality following the crash. We are also introduced to Carla's husband, Manny Rodrigo (Benicio Del Toro).

A psychiatrist, Dr. Bill Perlman (John Turturro), is provided by the airline to assist the passengers, many of whom will suffer post-traumatic syndrome. Max is a major victim of the emotional pain and is unable to go on with his once normal life.

Another character is Brillstein (Tom Hulce), a charming but sleazy lawyer bent on shaping the facts to include more pain and suffering for the deceased passengers and thus enhance the monetary judgments for surviving family members. Tom Hulce is brilliant in his portrayal, but for me, Hulce will forever be Mozart, no matter what his role. His performance in *Amadeus* was so unique it stamps each of his later performances with its image in the same way that *A Streetcar Named Desire* followed Marlon Brando throughout his career.

Rosie Perez's performance is clearly the most spectacular. We have seen her up to now as a wonderful comedienne. She demonstrates here that she is not limited to the comic and that she is simply a brilliant actress able to play any role.

Running as a constant threat through the movie is the unanswered question: Is Max Klein an extension of God? When I left I wasn't certain either way. But I was certain that I had enjoyed a wonderful movie with excellent actors.

A Few Good Men (+)

This is a fine movie. Not a great one, but it will hold your attention from start to finish. It would have been far better had it been subjected to a few good cuts.

It's not that the movie is too long. It's not. It's not that Demi Moore playing Tom Cruise's superior (Cruise plays a navy trial lawyer) isn't a fine actress. She is. But her role, like that of her counterpart in the original Broadway production, was not key to the play and was probably created to provide a possible love interest. However, there are no sensual, let alone sexual, scenes between Moore and Cruise. In fact, there was no chemistry between the two, and if she wasn't present in the flick, I assure you her character would not be missed.

Jack Nicholson is brilliant and dominates the screen even though he only appears three times. He is portrayed as perhaps you might envision Ollie North would be if faced with a command decision.

Nicholson has got to be a major contender for what I guess would be described as best supporting actor, although he dominates the film. I saw him recently at a dinner and told him I thought his performance was spectacular. He didn't disagree with me.

For the Boys (−)

For the Boys is, regrettably, for the birds. Bette Midler deserved a better vehicle to demonstrate her talents.

Midler is popular now, but it wasn't always that way. In her early days, she was the raunchiest cabaret artist, male or female, in the business. Midler combined that raunchiness with other appealing qualities, similar to what made Edith Piaf an extraordinary star. Piaf and the young Midler both had a vulnerable, gamine personality that made you want to protect them. It is interesting that the three women who I feel fit this bill—the third is Joan Rivers—are all so tiny and so gifted.

Bette Midler reached her zenith to date in *The Rose*, playing a drug-addicted singer. In that film she used her singing voice to exhibit her vulnerability, raunchiness and gamine quality.

With a major talent like Bette Midler as one of its leads, why doesn't *For the Boys* work? Its major flaw is that the screenwriters thought they had the writing skills of Tolstoy and were capable of covering three wars and about fifty years of history in one movie. They lacked the genius necessary to do it well. Midler and her costar James Caan, who are both normally first-rate, cannot carry this weak script, no matter how talented they are.

The Bette Midler I know was recently best revealed when she commented on Geraldo Rivera's autobiography which named her as one of his many sexual conquests. She responded as only she could, saying "He was a lousy lay." Bring back the one and only divine Miss M.

Glengarry Glen Ross (+)

This movie is a gem. Almost every frame on the screen is a close-up revealing the weaknesses and strengths of the characters and the ugliness to be found in a major sector of the world of commerce. The degradation of the characters—all salesmen—by their employer, a sleazy real estate company, owned by Mitch and Murray who never appear in the movie, is always sordid and at times heartbreaking.

The salesmen spend their time pitching—first on the phone and later, if they get lucky, at the victim's home—get-rich-quick land schemes to families who have no idea what they're buying and who cannot afford to lose the money they are investing in their foolish hope to get rich.

The movie opens with Alec Baldwin playing a killer salesman administrator sent from the front office to instill the fear of death—meaning termination of job—into a handful of these seedy salesmen whose sales are flagging. Baldwin is superb as he lauds his own material success—foreign car, gold watch, custom-made suit, six-figure income—over this pathetic group whose productive lives are nearly over and who are living from hand to mouth. The latter blame their past poor performance on the failure of the company to provide them with live "leads"—the names of people who have shown a prior interest in making land purchases.

Jack Lemmon as Shelley Levene carries the major role and is superb in portraying another more articulate version of Willie been revealed in the real life ongoing battle between Allen and Farrow.

The laughter was not derisive, but more like the nervous laughter we experience when we are present during a personally difficult situation involving our own families: almost like a sudden recollection of an earlier occurrence, painful or funny, coming once again into our consciousness.

The story involves husbands and wives and their lovers. The opening scene shows one of the couples, Judy (Mia Farrow) and Gabe (Woody Allen) in their apartment, it's a rather small rabbit warren that many of us who grew up in the Bronx or Brooklyn will recall, not the kind of spacious, architecturally interesting apartment we think of as being on the island of Manhattan; but this apartment is in Manhattan, the center of the world, and there are many like it.

Judy and Gabe's best friends Sally (Judy Davis) and Jack (Sydney Pollack) come over and announce at dinner that they are going to divorce after many years of marriage, with their children now grown. The news seems to devastate Judy the most.

From that point on we have the travails of Sally and Jack, each seeking new sexual and social relationships and finding it difficult to relate to their new social and sexual partners. Jack takes up with a very young woman, Sam (Lysette Anthony), who in olden days would be described as a sexpot. Sally starts seeing an editor named Michael (Liam Neeson).

Meanwhile Gabe, a professor teaching a writing course at Columbia, becomes involved with a young student, Rain (Juliette Lewis). You will recall Lewis as the pubescent adolescent in *Cape Fear*. She now plays an older nubile girl who wants Gabe as a lover. Judy ultimately splits with Gabe and begins a new relationship.

There is not a false note in the entire film. No matter what happens to Woody Allen during his current personal tragedy, we will always need him to explain New Yorkers to the world.

In the Line of Fire (+)

Finally, a movie that I can praise without reservation.

The plot is brilliant, involving a pathological situation between two deeply troubled men. One, Mitch Leary (John Malkovich), is truly nuts, a killer who wants to assassinate the president of the United States. The other, Frank Horrigan (Clint Eastwood), is a decent, troubled man who was one of the Secret Service men guarding President Kennedy at the very moment of his assassination in Dallas.

Malkovich's Mitch Leary is done in such a malevolent manner it will be hailed as one of the standards to judge pyschotic killer roles. Indeed, the only other two that rival it in my judgment are Richard Widmark in *Kiss of Death* (who would forget that insane laugh)?, and Anthony Hopkins as Hannibal (the cannibal) Lechter in *The Silence of the Lambs*. Malkovich makes his killer truly human and understandable through understatement.

The Indian Runner (+)

The Indian Runner is a flawed, but gripping movie. It is allegorical, mythic and powerful.

The allegory and myth come into play because it's the story of two brothers reminiscent of the biblical Cain and Abel. Joe (Abel), a cop played by David Morse, has a near angelic look with a fey approach to life while Frankie (Cain), played by Viggo Mortensen, is violent and in constant uncontrollable rage.

This film marks Sean Penn's directorial debut and he also wrote the script. Based on his public image when he was married to Madonna and involved in inexplicable violent episodes, one could speculate that he is exhibiting the demons and fury that lie within himself.

Penn has a great hand and eye with the camera. The landscape scenes, particularly the highways, are spectacular. Throughout the film the myth of *The Indian Runner*, the free spirit, appears. I don't understand what Penn sought to convey by using it, but it was not a distraction. The soundtrack featuring "Highway Patrolman" by Bruce Springsteen, and a number of other excellent numbers, is suberb and very moving.

Three cheers for Janet Maslin of the *New York Times*. We finally agreed on a movie.

The Inner Circle (+)

Filmed in Russia, where the picture is set, the cast consists of mostly Russian actors and two international stars, Tom Hulce, American, and Bob Hoskins, English.

The central figure is a projectionist played by Tom Hulce. He is brought to the Kremlin to become Stalin's pesonal projectionist a few years before the outbreak of World War II. Hulce is good, but his portrayal of Mozart in *Amadeus* was so powerful that almost anything he has done since suffers by comparison, including this role.

The projectionist lives in a squalid tenement with about six other families. The first sign of Stalinist oppression is seen when a Jewish couple living in the tenement is seized and ultimately executed, with their six-year-old daughter placed in an orphanage.

Hulce is newly married to a lovely young woman played by Lolita Davidovich, who wants to adopt the child. She is denounced by Hulce because the child after all is the child of traitors. He reveres Stalin and knows the consequences of consorting with enemies of the State. In an especially poignant scene Davidovich asks Hulce whom he loves more, her or Stalin. Hulce, without malice, replies, "Stalin, of course," conveying "What a silly question." But through his wife's later sufferings, which I will not reveal here, he realizes the brutality of Stalin and his government.

Years later, the orphaned girl meets Hulce. When he urges her to consider becoming a doctor, she says (even though she too has total faith in Stalin), "No, No, you know that is not possible. I am a Jew."

The cameo role played by Hoskins as Beria, the head of the KGB, is done brilliantly. He looks like Beria simply by the cast of the eye, with no apparent change in his physique or face. What a great actor!

The film does portray very grippingly Russia at war with Germany, using occasional newsreels to great advantage. It also gives us new insights into Russian society under Stalin. The mystique of Stalin overwhelmed millions of Russians who saw him as their father as well as their personal god. In the movie and undoubtedly in fact they referred to him as "Master." They rioted for the opportunity to see him in his casket fearful of what might now happen to Mother Russia. According to the film crawl, 1500 people died as a result of the crowd behavior.

Given the current turmoil in the new Commonwealth of Independent States, successor to the U.S.S.R., *The Inner Circle* is particularly moving and interesting.

JFK (+)

JFK is a marvelous picture. It reminds me of *Z* by Costa-Gavras. It is just as fast-paced and holds your interest every second; however, the background music in *Z* was far superior to that in *JFK*.

The movie succeeds despite the fact that this is probably Kevin Costner's worst performance; he plays the lead, former District Attorney Jim Garrison of New Orleans, who unsuccessfully prosecuted Clay Shaw, a New Orleans businessman, in

connection with JFK's assassination. His Southern accent grated on my ear and sounded totally false. When you compare it
with the Southern accent of Tommy Lee Jones, who plays
Shaw, it's like comparing wool to polyester: One's real, the
other counterfeit. Costner, as we all learned from *Robin Hood*, is
no Meryl Streep when it comes to accents.

Everyone knows the plot. The many questions raised by
Oliver Stone include: Who did it? Was there a conspiracy? Was
Oswald really the perpetrator? If so, did he act alone as concluded by the Warren Commission? And many more absorbing
and legitimate questions.

It is interesting that former DA Garrison, the heroic figure in
the film, has a cameo role playing Earl Warren, and in real life
was an appellate judge in Louisiana until his recent retirement.
Sissy Spacek, playing Garrison's wife, is wasted. Her role could
have been better played by dozens of actresses. She brought
nothing special to it, although she normally is a first-rate actress.

This movie is like a sledge hammer. What we need now is a
scalpel to do a real autopsy.

The Joy Luck Club (+)

This movie is epic in its proportions, depicting the lives of three
generations of women: four Chinese-American women now
living in San Francisco, their mothers who emigrated from
China and their grandmothers in China shown through flashbacks. The four younger women all live in family settings
which include their China-born mothers, who speak English
somewhat haltingly, but always eloquently. The lives of the
eight women (twelve, counting the grandmothers) are inter-
twined and demonstrate enormous courage in difficult situa-
tions both in China and the U.S.

The cast is enormous and, with a handful of exceptions, all
Asian. I've never seen a movie with as many memorable indi-

vidual performances. The actresses are all so good that it would be wrong to single one out. A recognition problem arises because there are so many characters involved. In addition to a story that reports on twelve different lives, the second and third generations are played at various times in their lives as children. So in many cases the same character is played by several people.

I had the feeling I was seeing a Chinese *East of Eden*. That film, too, was epic in its scope, depicting the America of early California days with James Dean as the second generation. There were a substantial number of Asians in the audience when I saw *The Joy Luck Club*, but this movie will be meaningful to any ethnic minority in the U.S. And it will appeal to those who enjoy what used to be called "a woman's movie." With our new androgynous outlook and likes, it will appeal to many men as well.

Juice (+)

Juice is very well done. It is much more a social commentary than a movie. As commentary, it's chilling. As a movie, superb entertainment. It provides a picture of black youth that, if true, should cause black families to weep for a lost generation totally out of touch with all decent societal norms.

Ernest Dickerson, the director, is brilliant. This movie and *Boyz N the Hood* are two of the best of this new genre. However, *Boyz N the Hood* left the viewer with hope that some of the youths depicted would overcome the terrible odds overwhelming their lives.

Juice, which in street talk means "power," as in "he's got the juice," the last words uttered in the film to one of the surviving gang members, leaves you totally bereft of hope. *Juice* paints a distorted picture of the black community because of its unending brutality and grimness. In fact, the black community has enormous problems, but enormous strengths as well.

Whenever 1915's *Birth Of A Nation*, now perceived as a movie classic, is shown there are pickets outside. The protesters feel the director, D.W. Griffith, portrayed blacks in the worst possible light. *Juice*, done by a black director and screenwriter with black actors, portrays black youths as monstrous. Nevertheless, it is applauded by many blacks and the movie shows signs of becoming a cult film.

Jurassic Park (−)

This movie is strictly for children, the ones who don't easily suffer trauma at the sight of a little blood and guts, and most won't.

The movie is a disaster for the moviegoers who stand in line for every show. For someone looking for the adventure and character portrayals done so well by Steven Spielberg in *Jaws* and *E.T.*—you won't find them here.

Using computers and other modern technology, Spielberg and company were able to create marvelously life-like creatures. They are much more natural looking than what we've been accustomed to in such movies as *One Million B.C.* with Victor Mature, but so what? The technological genius generates mental applause when you see the dinosaurs (by the way, one looks like the critters from *Gremlins*), but that's five minutes of a movie that is two hours in length.

Throughout the movie all I could think of was how much better *King Kong* was over fifty years ago in creating a sense of reality, love, fear and an appreciation for a huge animal that had 5 percent of the technical proficiency of the animals portrayed in this film.

If you really want to see a movie that played with Mother Nature and DNA before any of us ever heard of DNA, you should rent *Island of Lost Souls* and the remake *The Island of Dr. Moreau*, where people were turned into animals by a fiendish doctor. The original starred Charles Laughton and the remake Burt Lancaster. My recollection is that the island on which it all occurred was set ablaze at the end of the movie. Regrettably, as *Jurassic Park* ends, our human friends all escape by helicopter, but the dinosaurs remain alive and well, reproducing and getting ready for the sequel.

The Last Boy Scout (–)

This is the worst movie I have ever seen. Of course, I didn't see *Hudson Hawk*. I can't imagine why Bruce Willis—who was brilliant in the *Die Hard* pictures—made this film, unless it was for the money.

I like action films. I'm not appalled by violence, blood or guts, as long as they're not mine and make sense, but this movie is senseless. It is violent, yet nevertheless will cause you to yawn and pinch yourself so that you don't fall asleep. The plot is too inane to waste any comment or critique.

Those of you who are warned off by this review, you owe me!

Let's Fall in Love (+)

I found this documentary film involving, perhaps because I've participated in the scene described: A singles weekend at the Concord Hotel in the Catskills.

The cameras interview men and women who are mostly in their forties, but some are older. All speak unaffectedly and interestingly about their feelings about being at the Concord looking to find someone, either for a date or maybe to marry. The obvious difficulties for almost all are candidly discussed: The need to project, to be interesting, to overcome the disconcerting fact that, while you are engaged in conversation with a newly-met possible partner for the evening, he or she is constantly looking the room over to see if there is someone better (whatever "better" means).

One woman says, "I want him to keep looking me in the eye as he's talking to me and treat me like a person." One man, fearful of showing too much interest in a woman he met at the bar, tells the camera he walked away early so as not to seem too eager. He then spent the next twenty-four hours looking for her, only to find she had found a new attachment. As he wistfully describes it, he saw the new couple—headed back to either the girl's or the guy's room.

One of the men says he's been to singles weekend five times in the last few years—and will keep coming. It must be painful for most and there must be a better way. Nevertheless, you have to admire their spunk and willingness to reveal so much of themselves. It is not the best of movies, and certainly a Woody Allen flick on the same subject (and most are) provides more enjoyment, but this movie has a charm and an interest that makes it thought provoking.

Lovers (+)

Lovers is just that, a story of a young farm boy, Paco, who is discharged from the Spanish army in the mid 1950s and who is in love with two women (Franco is still the Caudillo, Prime Minister, of Spain).

The women are totally different from one another, Trini (Maribel Verdu) is a young, innocent woman working as a maid who can hardly wait for Paco (Jorge Sanz) to return to her after his discharge; when he does she is demurely put off by his sexual advances.

Paco finds lodgings in a bed and breakfast apartment run by an older woman, Luisa (Victoria Abril). At their first meeting, Luisa takes him to bed and introduces him to sophisticated sexual practices that are new to him, but which he takes to like a duck to water. Each of the women is angered and thinks of revenge when they learn of the other's involvement.

Luisa is a con artist and steals from one of her criminal associates. She is threatened by them and told she must replace the stolen money or have her beautiful face destroyed. To save herself, she enlists Paco in a scheme to defraud Trini of her modest savings. I will not reveal who ultimately succeeds in winning exclusive rights to Paco's love, but the picture ends in a tragedy with the credit crawl revealing what happened to the survivors.

The movie is based on a real life story and it spins the tale beautifully with torrid lovemaking, nudity and enough schmerz and angst for three pictures. The actors are all very competent and physically attractive.

The scenes of Spain, particularly those of a town outside of Madrid, are a pleasure to see. They reminded me of how much I enjoyed vacationing in Spain, especially because of the warmth of its people, the superb food and the grandeur of its cathedrals, museums and antiquities.

Malcolm X (+)

This is a fine film. While it undoubtedly has special meaning and poignancy for blacks, just as the movie *Exodus* had for Jews, the story of this man is so gripping it will hold the attention of all despite the fact that it's three hours and twenty minutes long.

Director Spike Lee did a superb job of bringing together the disparate parts of Malcolm X's life using a script based on Alex Haley's *The Autobiography of Malcolm X*. Malcolm was born with the "slave" name Malcolm Little. His mother, Louise (Lonette McKee), was the child of a black woman raped by a white man and his father, Earl (Tommy Hollis), was a well-educated black minister.

Early on, Malcolm was initiated into the awful dangers facing blacks—or Negroes in those days—particularly when local bigots (in this case, Ku Klux Klan riders) perceived his daddy as "uppity." That term is not used in the movie, but was often used in earlier films and criminal trials involving assaults by whites against blacks to describe Negroes whom the "locals" believed should be put in their place. Malcolm's father is ultimately murdered for his independence.

The film's opening scene takes place in Harlem with flashbacks to Malcolm's childhood. In that first scene we see Spike Lee, a street hustler named Shorty, in a flamboyant outfit worthy of *Guys And Dolls*, walking down the avenue with Malcolm X (Denzel Washington) in similar garish attire. They strut like peacocks before the girls. Spike Lee, the director, does well choreographing dance hall numbers that admirers of Busby Berkeley would enjoy. You've never seen the jitterbug done better.

Then we see Malcolm X on his way to jail after committing a burglary. In jail, he is converted by a follower of the Nation of Islam and becomes a Muslim. Early on he has a love affair with a young woman named Betty (Angela Bassett) who later becomes his wife and whom we know as his widow, Betty Shabazz, who now teaches at Medgar Evers College. The chemistry, true love and friendship between them and their three daughters is beautifully captured on the screen by Washington and Bassett.

Ultimately, Malcolm X becomes the number one minister in the Nation of Islam and is perceived as a danger to other ministers who envy his success with the media. These ministers seek successfully to turn the Hon. Elijah Muhammad against Malcolm X. Elijah Muhammad is played superbly by Al Freeman Jr. It is remarkable how both Washington and Freeman bring to mind the men they are portraying with their voices and mannerisms.

The final assassination scene is truly outstanding in drama, excitement and choreography. Spike Lee sets the scene with conversations between Malcolm X and his wife and followers, that make clear he senses his impending death and accepts it. He says he believes he is the target not only of the Nation of Islam, but also of agents of the federal government.

Indeed, during the movie he is trailed by two white men and his telephone is tapped. One tapper says to the other, "He lives the life of a saint compared to King," Whether or not this is historically accurate, I don't know. But it was in the era of J. Edgar Hoover and we know that the FBI did trail and tap the phones of Martin Luther King Jr.

Now that the government is releasing all its files on the assassination of President Kennedy, they ought to do the same on the assassinations of Bobby Kennedy, Martin Luther King Jr. and Malcolm X because in each case, the zealots (who may or may not be right) continue to weave conspiracy theories that receive additional credibility because the government does not make all the records public. Malcolm X was assassinated and three members of the Nation of Islam were tried and sent to jail. They never admitted to any conspiracy involving the Nation of Islam with respect to this assassination.

Whether or not Malcolm X had an epiphany as a result of his Haj to Mecca and renounced his hostility towards whites is in dispute. The picture makes clear he did, but I've heard commentators who believe his changeover is vastly overstated. However, his letters that are read on screen would indicate he had given up his hostility to whites, after having met with white Muslims in Mecca who treated him as a brother.

In any event, his friends and admirers, and I'm an admirer, believe his legacy is now a force for good and he probably has the same standing in the black community's pantheon of heroes that Martin Luther King has. When I was mayor I renamed two streets in Malcolm X's honor, one in Brooklyn and one in Harlem.

I recommend this picture particularly during this time of escalating black and white hostility. It can bring better understanding of what it meant and means to be black in an over-whelmingly white country where race is still the dominant and unaddressed issue.

Malice (−)

I'm sorry folks, but this is another stinker. The promos looked good, but I am never moved by them, since I know they rarely have anything to do with the flick. But this time I had the additional comment of a friend who had seen it and said, while it was "a junk film," it was also interesting. It was not.

It had a string of subplots that you could find on afternoon soap operas. Except television does them better.

It is basically a mystery and who-done-it movie. Such movies are hard to review, because the reviewer must never give away the plot and all the diversions intended to throw you off the scent. Let me try to walk between the mines and shoals and still provide a broad outline of the movie.

The film opens on a college campus in Boston. We are soon privy to several killings, and quickly realize there is a serial killer on campus. We meet Tracy (Nicole Kidman) who in real life is the wife of Tom Cruise. In the movie, she is the wife of Andy (Bill Pullman), a dean of students, and she takes pills for the piercing pains that she complains of in her abdomen. We are also introduced to Dr. Jed Hill (Alec Baldwin), who has just joined the staff of St. Agnes Hospital. He is a crackerjack surgeon. He becomes involved with our apparently happily married couple and moves into the third floor of their Victorian house.

There are some steamy sex scenes in the bedroom of the married couple, and not only the audience watches. There are no drapes on the windows and anyone across the way with a prurient interest can witness the coupling. There is a young boy, who we learn is ill (he's constantly playing the piano), intently gazing across the alley separating the two houses.

The couple's boarder. Dr. Hill, is also into torrid love making, enough to make the bed and floor shake, causing discomfort to Tracy and Andy, who are sleeping, or, more likely, entwined immediately below.

The balance of the film deals with: a botched operation by our spectacular doctor; a lawsuit for malpractice; an examination before trial that exhibits the skills of Peter Gallagher as Tracy's lawyer and George C. Scott as an expert witness; the discovery of the serial killer's identity; a runaway wife and a lonely house perched on top of a hill reminiscent of *Psycho*.

I only wish this movie had the panache of *Psycho*. While there are moments of fear created by the use of clichés and various settings, particularly as Andy wanders around a cellar looking for a fuse and finds instead someone who may or may not be the serial killer, they aren't enough to make sitting through this creaking, Grade B thriller worthwhile.

The acting is okay on the part of all the principals, but no better than okay. Those interested in seeing Kidman and Baldwin undressed may think the movie worthwhile. If they do, they are paying a lot—$7.50—for very little.

Married to It (+)

About two years ago, I had lunch with an old friend, Tom Baer, a Hollywood film producer. He brought along Arthur Hiller, a director. Hiller asked if I would be interested in playing myself in a movie, a very small part but one that I would enjoy—it had a few lines and the scene took place at Gracie Mansion. Of course, I said yes immediately.

The six stars, not including me, are Stockard Channing, Beau Bridges, Mary Stuart Masterson, Robert Sean Leonard, Cybill Shepherd and Ron Silver. Every one of them did an excellent job, was believable in their roles and provided a very enjoyable two hours.

around a tree which they decorate with candles and a hand grenade. The Americans provide the wine from the abandoned chateau and the Germans provide schnapps and wurst.

While the proposed surrender of the German squad to the six Americans has been carefully choreographed, fate plays a role and a firefight breaks out with tragic consequences just as the German offensive begins. The Americans attempt to withdraw to the American lines in their jeeps, but they find headquarters empty and run out of gas as they see the SS troops advancing. They are now behind enemy lines. The young sergeant decides they must devise a plan to stay alive and get back to their own lines. The unique plan they come up with and its execution is an especially memorable section of the film.

The most poignant scene for me was the washing of the body of the deceased American soldier, killed by the Germans during the firefight, by the remaining members of the squad. The soldier's body, stiff with rigor mortis, looks like the crucified Christ. The scene evoked memories of the mandatory Jewish obligation that every dead person be washed before being interred. This scene and the Christmas celebration scene were remarkably devoid of sentimentality and bathos.

This is a superb film that makes a powerful anti-war statement. It rivals two of the greatest anti-war films: *All Quiet On the Western Front* and *Slaughterhouse Five*. I saw the movie on a Tuesday evening at the Plaza at 58th St. and Fifth Ave. which was a good-sized screen. I was surprised that, in spite of superb reviews, the theater was only about 30 percent full. If you miss this movie, you're missing a winner.

Mr. Saturday Night (+)

This is a movie that relies on nostalgia for its success, and it works. It will certainly work for New York Jews who will see their childhoods reflected in the childhood of Buddy (Billy Crystal) and his brother Stan (David Paymer).

The brief scenes of family dinners strike a particularly poignant note. The food served at those dinners violated every current medical rule, especially those prohibiting fat and salt, not to mention the humungous portions. Those meals were enough to kill you on the spot or at least guarantee a shortened life. The people Crystal (who also directed the film) assembled could have been my relatives—or yours.

You'll also see the borscht belt revues that you attended as I did at Grossinger's, the Concorde, Brown's and Kutsher's. It will bring back your recollections of living at a "Kochalain" (although not depicted in the film) where you had your bedroom, shared a kitchen with four other families, but cooked (Kochalain) on your own burner and marked your food in the common refrigerator; at night you paid a small fee to enter the casino at a nearby hotel to see the great comedians Red Buttons, Milton Berle or Jerry Lewis, or hear the great singers Sammy Davis, Tony Martin or Dinah Shore and so many more.

This movie traces the life of a composite comedian, who could have been any of the above or six others whose names I have forgotten. The relationship between the comedian and his brother are at the heart of the film. The younger brother, Buddy, the comedian, is the more gifted artistically; the other Stan, less so, becomes his business agent. Buddy has an overwhelming ego. It is that ego that ultimately destroys him: His talent is not that great and with frustration his act becomes less acceptable as he becomes more lewd and caustic in his attacks on his audience.

David Paymer gives the best performance as the older brother who is treated outrageously by his more successful younger brother, but cannot leave him out of family loyalty.

A severe flaw in the movie was Crystal's makeup as an older Buddy. It rivalled that of Bette Midler's in the geriatric scenes in *For the Boys*: horrible. On the other hand, David Paymer's aging makeup was fine, aging him with real character lines remaining on his face. If the same person did both faces it is inexplicable.

Mistress (−)

I had heard good things about this flick. I've never seen De Niro in a bad movie. This is a first, although he, and the rest of the cast, performed superbly.

The plot: An elderly, down-on-his-luck talent agent, Jack Roth (Martin Landau), finds an old script which he thinks has great possibilities. Then we see the script's writer, Marvin Landisman, (Robert Wuhl), who is holed up in his apartment watching *Grand Illusion*.

Landisman tells Roth when he calls that, yes, he will meet him at some seedy burger cafe in Hollywood to discuss making his script into a movie. Roth brings along an obnoxious young scriptwriter, Stuart Stratland (Jace Alexander). Landisman protests a dozen times that he will not compromise a word of the script. And when told that a possible investor, George Lieberhoff (Eli Wallach), will want his girlfriend in the movie, he sputters that he won't take her and then, almost immediately in his first compromise, says, "Unless she has talent."

Ultimately there are three investors, all of whom want their girlfriends similarly featured. Danny Aiello plays one of them and his performance, along with that of Jean Smart as his mistress, is spectacular. And finally, enter De Niro, who gives a dazzling performance as does the actress playing his mistress, Sheryl Lee Ralph, a young black woman with enormous presence, both emotional and physical.

From that point on the film deals with the ultimate failure of all involved in getting the film produced. The earlier viewers leaving the movie when we arrived were absolutely right. "It should have been a great movie"—but it wasn't. I'm not sure why, but all I know is that I was bored by it and occasionally drifted off to sleep (but only for a moment or two, after all I was on duty). At the same time two members of my party, G.K. and H.K., liked it, but with some reservations. H.K. said, "Where the picture failed was in its cynical, dismal view of the future. Where it succeeded was in the acting."

My Own Private Idaho (–)

My Own Private Idaho centers around two male hustlers, Mike and Scott, played by River Phoenix and Keanu Reeves. It was, undoubtedly, produced to attract both a homosexual and heterosexual audience. The coupling—male and female—is done so demurely that it will not raise the blood pressure of any spectator.

Reeves's character is the son of the town's wheelchair-bound mayor. He is secure in his gay lifestyle and constantly flaunts it to anger his father, apparently wanting to embarrass him to death; he ultimately succeeds.

Phoenix plays another gay hustler who is more confused and less confident. He does tricks regularly with male customers and an occasional female. He looks as seedy as you would expect any young man living on the streets would.

At the beginning of the movie there is some verbal interplay between Reeves, Phoenix and a motley crew of vagrants employing Shakespearean language with references to Falstaff. Only the director, Gus Van Sant Jr., and his psychiatrist could possibly understand its purpose.

Reeves and Phoenix meet and become friends as they go on the road together searching for Phoenix's runaway mother.

There is one poignant scene, not overtly physically sexual, in which Phoenix confesses his love for Reeves. At first, Reeves rejects him, conveying that he is not capable of love without being paid for it, but then he reaches out and cradles Phoenix in his arms. Phoenix is an excellent actor and Reeves holds his own, but this is a disappointing film. Skip it.

One False Move (+)

One False Move is a good one. One caveat: if you don't like explicit violence on the screen, this is a movie to avoid. It's like kill, kill, kill all summer long.

The plot involves two men and a woman who are out to make their fortune by ripping off drug dealers. The opening scene depicts one such rip-off with the threesome employing the well-known M.O. of Colombian drug lords, which is to murder everyone in the apartment including the children so that there are no witnesses. One of the trio is a young black man, Pluto (Michael Beach), who is the leader and is exceedingly cruel. The other male, Ray (Billy Bob Thornton, who co-wrote the screenplay) is a white psycho who mistreats the female member of the trio, his lover, Fantasia (Cynda Williams), a woman whose mother was black and whose father was white. It is Fantasia who gains entry for them into the homes of drug pushers with whom she apparently has close friendships.

The opening killings take place in Los Angeles and from that point on the criminals are on the run travelling to Arkansas and Texas. All of these places look alike to me. If they didn't identify the towns with English subtitles, all I would know is that they are west of the Bronx.

The L.A. cops, who are in hot pursuit, contact a local sheriff, Dale "Hurricane" Dixon (Bill Paxton), in a small Arkansas town. Dixon is an attractive young man, sort of a cross between a hillbilly and a would-be preppy. Dixon idolizes the L.A. police force, and their detectives (competently portrayed by Jim Metzler and Earl Billings) who play him like a trout in a stream while snickering at his clumsiness from their police and forensic point of view.

Ultimately it is the hillbilly sheriff who brings the criminals to bay in a violent shoot-out. There are seductive scenes between him and Fantasia who seeks through her sexual wiles to induce him to free her from custody.

The movie probably cost next to nothing to make and will become a cult film. It's worth seeing and it's worth getting to know the Film Forum so as to become aware of its repertoire of classic films as well as off-beat new ones.

The Player (+)

A wonderful movie for most, including me. But some moviegoers may not enjoy it as much because they may feel, as one member of my party, D.M., said, "It was like turning the pages of a magazine with no connection and difficult to stay involved."

The director, Robert Altman, was bent on showing Hollywood, from bad to worse, from warts to cancer. It is a very broad satire, at times a near burlesque of the entire community of agents, actors, writers and most of all the top movie studio executives. I say satire and burlesque because it's hard to believe an industry could be as banal, petty and corrupt from top to bottom as depicted. But maybe it is and surely Altman, who's directed dozens of movies including "*M*A*S*H*" and *Nashville*, knows what he is doing.

In *The Player*, Tim Robbins is a sophisticated movie executive who has to decide which scripts, of the thousands received every year, the studio should put millions of dollars into making. During this process of rejecting scripts—and his practice is to allow a twenty-five-word pitch (his word for the process) by the writer to sell him—he has angered one rejected writer who is now sending him threatening postcards which escalate to death threats. Griffin tries to identify the writer and find him. In the course of seeking to free himself from these threats, he unintentionally kills a suspect.

For the next hour you are at the edge of your seat while the movie takes you on a tour of the Hollywood scene, lavish homes, parties, restaurants, and a spa, allowing the audience and Robbins to determine whether the murdered script writer is the one who sent the threatening notes. Altman was able to get Julia Roberts, Burt Reynolds, Cher, Harry Belafonte, Bruce Willis and dozens of other actors to appear in what amounts to less than cameo roles (most have no lines at all, some one or two sentences), but seeing them this way is lots of fun for us and maybe for them as well.

One full length cameo is by Whoopi Goldberg who plays the detective investigating the murder. She is one of the great comediennes of our age. She does a schtick with tampons that will have you rolling in the aisle. The denouement which takes the last five minutes of the film provides the most fun of all, but getting to it includes scenes of passion as well as tepid nudity by both Robbins and Greta Scacchi, who plays Robbins' love interest.

It is clear that Altman was bent on satirizing every Hollywood and L.A. schtick and cliché. He made L.A. or LaLa land squirm—or appreciate how strange they look to the rest of us. I enjoyed each page of the magazine.

The Prince of Tides (+)

The Prince of Tides is good, but not as good as the hype.

Like Woody Allen's *Manhattan*, during the New York scenes we see Manhattan in all its wonder: The heart of New York City never looked better. There are also some lovely moments on the beaches of South Carolina. When considered separately from the rest of the film, these scenes are a memorable delight.

The story line involves growing up in the white South as part of a family with three lovely children and two parents; the parents slowly destroy one another and create neuroses in the children that will dominate their adult lives. These neuroses manifest themselves when one of the now grown children, Savannah, played by Melinda Dillon, attempts suicide. Savannah, a famous poet, has been seeing a psychiatrist, Dr. Lowenstein (Barbra Streisand), and Savannah's brother, Tom (Nick Nolte), travels from the South to New York to meet with Lowenstein and probe his sister's problems.

The story quickly degenerates into a soap opera with the psychiatrist recognizing that the basic cause of Savannah's (and Tom's) problems are rooted in their childhood. She attempts to uncover the truth by probing Nolte's memory with daily analytic sessions with Nolte as an unwilling analysand.

And, of course, the core incident that has caused the problem, turns out to be a sexual trauma suffered by Nolte and his family. This revelation gives Nolte the opportunity to break down emotionally in a scene that some critics say could earn him an Academy Award. He reaches for the comfort of the psychiatrist's arms and hands; she urges him to let it all out and not hold back his tears. Unlocking that memory, of course, changes the course of all the lives involved—just like real life, no?

The love affair that develops between Nolte and Streisand is quite tame, considering their obviously tempestuous natures. There is no nudity and it's all very civilized with a really idyllic scene at the country estate of the psychiatrist.

Several reviews have commented on Streisand as a director, usually acclaiming her, with almost all mentioning a tendency toward self-indulgence on her part. They always mention that time after time the cinema focuses on her beautifully crafted legs. She does have well turned out ankles and calves, but I believe she is also a little knock-kneed.

The film also features Streisand's real life son, Jason Gould, who plays her son in the movie. He does a very credible job. Some of the best acting is done by Nolte's mother, Kate Nelligan, who suffered so much herself because of her husband's violent nature. Equally great is Blythe Danner who portrays Nolte's Southern wife realistically and with much charm. Nolte and Streisand are both good, but not great. The soap opera script greatly limits what they can do.

Reservoir Dogs (+)

Most people will not enjoy this movie, despite its critical acclaim. It is the most violent movie I have ever seen. It must rival in gore and sadism the Grand Guignol of France. Never-theless, it is a masterpiece of the genre. The movie most akin to it would be *Straw Dogs* by Sam Peckinpah, another masterpiece of blood and gore.

The plot involves a group of five thugs bent on robbing a jewelry store. The leader is Joe Cabot (Lawrence Tierney), the father of another member of the gang, Nice Guy Eddie (Chris Penn). They bring together three other thugs who don't know one another and Cabot assigns each of them a pseudonym rep-resenting colors: Mr. White, Mr. Brown. When he dubs one guy (Steve Buscemi) Mr. Pink, he protests saying, "Why are you assigning me Pink? I want to be Mr. White or Mr. Brown." Cabot replies, "You're a fag and that's why you're Mr. Pink." That is the nature of the language, and it all rings true.

The robbery goes awry with one of the gang shot and killed at the scene and another wounded seriously while fleeing—but they do get away with the diamonds. When they begin to trick-le in at that rendezvous point, one of them, Mr. Blonde (Michael Madsen), brings a cop with him who has been taken hostage. The gang realizes that they must have been set up in some way because the cops were on the scene and apparently aware of the planned heist. Mr. Blonde, clearly a sadistic psy-chopath, begins to torture the young cop and these scenes are the most gruesome you will ever witness on the screen.

It would make no sense to further describe the plot because if you see this movie the reason you are there is to feel the sus-pense—minute by minute—as you watch the bloody plot unfold before you. Each scene is executed like a ballet: all the characters' movements are carefully choreographed.

Michael Madsen is extraordinary as the sadistic Mr. Blonde, as is Tim Roth as Mr. Orange, the youngest-looking member of the gang who is shot while running away from the botched robbery. There is an interesting unfulfilled homoerotic relation-ship between him and Mr. White (Harvey Keitel). Keitel and the other actors all turn in excellent performances.

No one in my party liked it other than me. Indeed, they all wanted to leave early on they were so disgusted. But I whispered, "I can't—this is my job," and like a good trooper M.B. stayed the course; B.B. and V.B. spent the last hour of the film waiting in the lobby.

A River Runs Through It (+)

Visually, this movie is incomparable; but regrettably, the storyline and drama required to make it totally engrossing are missing. The blue sky country of Montana will surely be the next vacation destination of those able to afford the airfare and who have the time for a leisurely trip. For most New Yorkers, the sport of fly fishing for rainbow trout will remain a video dream (for me it's a deadly boring sport) and they will settle for Washington, Connecticut or Green County, New York. The magnificent images of the river, the mountains and the pastures dominate the film.

In the movie crawl at the end we are told that none of the fish caught were injured or killed: Would it have been sinful had they been eaten by the extras?

Romeo Is Bleeding (–)

This is a movie totally devoted to violence. It has no redeeming value. In the last several years, violent movies of this genre have been overwhelmingly black with respect to all of the artists—actors, directors, and producers. I have criticized some of them, particularly the highly touted *Menace II Society*, as worthless if not harmful.

This movie, with a white male director, a white female screenwriter and all white actors, while having a camp humor quality to it, is similarly devoid of any legitimate interest for audiences. While I am opposed to restrictions being placed on what can be shown for adult viewing on television and in movies, I do believe that much of the material devoted to violence for violence's sake alone—much of which is cruel and misogynistic—can and does have an adverse impact on viewers. Preventing minors from viewing the material is primarily the job of parents and, in the case of movie houses, enforcing rating codes.

Romeo Is Bleeding is the story of a corrupt cop named Jack (Gary Oldham) who is married to Natalie (Annabella Sciorra) and also has a steady girlfriend, Sherri (Juliette Lewis). Jack is being paid off by organized crime figures who want him to locate mob informants under government protection so that the mob can have them rubbed out.

Jack arrests Mona (Lena Olin), a mob queen who is a threat to the don, Don Falcone (Roy Scheider). Mona has the ability to entice men sexually through her raw sensuality and by performing acts of physical violence such as garroting them with wires.

In one scene, Mona gains physical control by locking her legs in a vise-like grip around the neck of her victim while she is handcuffed in the backseat of a car, reminiscent of the super-woman depicted in *La Femine Nikita*. But Nikita, played by Anne Parillaud, was younger and more beautiful than Lena Olin and that picture had class; this movie has anything but class.

I could recount the shootings and murders, not to mention the numerous amputations—not quite rivaling *The Texas Chainsaw Massacre*—but that would ruin the viewing pleasure of those foolish enough to go to this film.

In what may have been a first, everyone with me agreed this film should be avoided. But judging from the lines at the theater, it will be doing business for quite some time to come.

M.B. said, "Silly; stupid."

B.M. said, "Pretentious."

D.M. said, "I'm hardpressed to recall a more preposterous film."

B.B., "That's because there has never been a more preposterous film."

J.S., "I kept wondering what part they were going to cut off next."

A.S., "Occasionally interesting, but excessively flawed."

Romper Stomper (−)

This movie is the Australian version of *Menace II Society* and just as appalling. Made and acted by Australians, it depicts a side of Australia you'll never want to see again.

Some critics have compared this movie to Stanley Kubrick's *A Clockwork Orange*. Nothing can be further from the truth. *A Clockwork Orange* was a brilliant look into the future. This movie is apparently an examination of the present and, like its American counterpart *Menace*, not worth looking at.

The story follows the doings of a gang of skinheads in Melbourne. The early part of the film deals with their attacks on Vietnamese immigrants, who are depicted as leading hard but productive lives. The skinheads set upon them simply because they are Asians or, as the skinheads refer to them, "gooks." Their very presence in a bar or anywhere else enrages the skinheads, who are depicted as Nazi lovers, have Nazi tattoos and wear Nazi gear.

One character, Hando (Russell Crowe), even speaks German. He has a tryst with a skinhead auxiliary, Gabe (Jacqueline McKenzie). Gabe hates her family, suffers from what appears to be epilepsy, and wants her loving to be very physical. She likes to be slapped around by those who sexually use her. Another auxiliary (my term) looks like a carbon copy of Boy George before he took off the make-up.

The mayhem and violence, comprised mostly of vicious beatings with occasional murders, includes the robbery of a wealthy older man. We later find out he has a surprising and deep interest in Gabe. I won't bother to describe any more of the skinheads or the actors because, for the most part, all the skinheads look alike, act alike, beat and kill and are beaten and killed alike, so why bother with names. If you are lucky you'll never see them again, at least in comparable roles: Why bother adding unnecessary information to your brain's memory chip.

Scent of a Woman (−)

This is a vastly overrated movie.

The script is ridiculous, except for the germ of an idea. It centers around a retired Lt. Col. blinded in a training accident who cannot accept his physical condition and wants one more fling on the town before he takes his life. The movie seeks to construct a relationship between this Lt. Col. Frank Slade (Al Pacino), and a prep school student, Charlie Simms (Chris O'Donnell). Charlie has problems of his own; an "aid" student from Oregon hoping to go on to Harvard, he is the object of his headmaster's ire and the victim of his rich classmates' actions.

Everything is predictable: It becomes a full-blown soap opera. Pacino's acting is atrocious and never more than one note, consisting mainly of his barking orders and screaming at O'Donnell's character. O'Donnell is not a bad actor and does convey diffidence and intelligence. But he is no more than adequate and cannot be expected to carry this picture.

Having put this movie down, let me tell you I was surprised that at the end there was a substantial burst of applause from the audience. M.B. said, "I'm not saying I liked it, but there were some moments." I didn't experience a single moment of exhilaration in spending the first night of the New Year watching this amateurish performance and script. Avoid if possible.

Schindler's List (+)

This is not the definitive film on the Holocaust. That is yet to be made. This film is certainly worth seeing, but it did not satisfy me emotionally.

Some critics, while praising the film, criticized the scenes depicting the brutality and horror visited upon the Jews by the Nazis. I believe that without those wrenching scenes this film would have little going for it. What is missing are scenes of interpersonal relationships.

I have seen many films on the Shoah, the Hebrew word for Holocaust. Each added to my store of knowledge. Each made me weep. Each conveyed the personal tragedy even if, as was the case in the films *The Sorrow and the Pity* and *Shoah*, the film makers avoided showing graphic atrocities against the Jews, but instead recounted them through the voices of the survivors.

On the other hand, *Europa, Europa*, the true story of an adolescent Jewish boy who lived through the Holocaust, did recount his suffering, if not day by day, almost year by year. For me *Europa. Europa* had the greatest impact of all the films of this genre to date.

Schindler's List, a true story of a Nazi German businessman who saved Jews, did not move me as those other films did. I was interested in what happened, but never identified with any of the Jewish victims depicted as I had expected. I wanted to identify with those victims, but neither the script nor the acting took me from my seat in the theater to a place on the screen. The movie by design failed to personalize the tragedies as they unfolded.

Schindler's initial motivation for employing Jews in his factory, which first manufactured pots and pans for the Wehrmacht and later war materials, was purely economic since it was cheaper than using Polish workers. Later he employed them to save their lives because he was shaken by the random acts of happening not at the shvitz baths, but while watching my aunts and older relatives bathing—not swimming—in the waters off Coney Island. It's an indelible memory.

Occasionally, this film conjured up other memories, but not enough. Some old news clips of the early days are inserted into the film from time to time. They are interesting, but not so interesting as to lift this film to a higher plane. The recollections of those interviewed are neither sufficiently personal nor historical enough to hold your interest for long. This was an interesting idea that failed in the execution.

For Jews it may be considered a walk down memory lane.

Short Cuts (−)

This film is guilty of short weight. It promised a lot (the pre-opening reviews were sensational), and delivered little.

I went to the film's first commercial showing—it had received rave reviews earlier as part of the New York Film Festival—on Sunday at 11 A.M. There was a line when I got there at 10:30. As I entered the darkened theater, I was greeted by a man about my age who looked familiar, but I didn't know who he was. I didn't get his name until he repeated it and added. "So, Mayor, you've come to see my film." I quickly recouped and said, "Mr. Altman, I hear great things about this film, and I'm here to review it." Smiling, he said, "Oh." And I added, "I'm sure I'll love it." Regrettably, I didn't. As I left I hoped he wouldn't be there saying good-bye, and he wasn't.

What's wrong with this film? I speak now of the missing pleasure, not the missing technical bravura. I'm sure the experts have pointed out the artistic brilliance in this production. That, as you know, is not my schtick.

The film seeks to weave together ten or so different stories concerning twenty-two characters. There is no real common thread holding them all together, except that most of the characters, generally couples, both married and not, are dysfunctional: some more, some less. It's hard to keep all of the couples separate in your head, but fortunately the producers gave everyone a beautiful score card with names and characters, without which I would be at a terrible loss. Some performances are stronger than others, although the acting is excellent throughout.

Tragedy strikes one couple, Howard Finnigan (Bruce Davison) and his wife, Ann (Andie MacDowell), when their son is hit by a car driven by Doreen Piggot (Lily Tomlin) and severely injured. The Finnigan marriage seems to be the least rocky and the least interesting except for the car injuries. Jack Lemmon appears as the grandfather of the boy and does a superb job.

Piggot, a waitress, is having a very difficult time with her husband, Earl (Tom Waits), who is an alcoholic. Sherri Sheppard (Madeleine Stowe) is having a fine sex life with Gene Shepard (Tim Robbins), an L.A. motorcycle cop who is very horny. Gene is looking to have extramarital sexual liaisons and tries to pick up Claire Kane (Anne Archer) on the freeway on the pretext that she is driving too slowly.

Claire Kane, who hires herself out as a clown, is married to Stuart (Fred Ward). Remember Ward? He played Henry Miller in *Henry and June* and did a splendid job. Serendipitiously, the night before seeing *Short Cuts* I had dinner at De Niro's Tribeca Grill. Ward arrived at the same time as I did and we shook hands while waiting to be seated. Only in New York.

Ward's character, Stuart Kane, is one of the boys, an angry, out of work salesman who, in one of the movie's many digressions, goes on a fishing trip with two buddies—Vern Miller (Huey Lewis) and Gordon Johnson (Buck Henry)—and finds a nude woman floating dead in the river.

A really bizarre couple is Betty (Frances McDormand) and Stormy Weathers (Peter Gallagher), who played the original Sky Masterson in the brilliant Broadway revival of *Guys & Dolls*. Weathers is a truly out-of-his-skull husband who is separated from his wife and viciously jealous of her dating other men.

Then there is Honey Bush (Lili Taylor), married to Bill Bush (Robert Downey, Jr.). He is a special effects make-up man who gets his wife to model for a gruesome murder scene he's working on. There is a fine performance from another woman twosome, Jerry (Chris Penn) and Lois Kaiser (Jennifer Jason Leigh), whose role is hilarious and nearly steals the movie. She is a telephone porno operator who talks really dirty to her callers.

Then there are Tess Tainer (Annie Ross), who plays a jazz singer, and her daughter Zoe (Lori Singer), a cellist who is extraordinarily sensitive. You know from the start that she will go off the deep end, and she does. Dr. Ralph Wyman (Matthew Modine) treats the Finnigan's injured son and is himself tormented because his wife, Marian Wyman (Julianne Moore), had an affair three years before and up until now has declined to give him the details he wants. Finally there is Lyle Lovett, who plays a disturbed banker who enters the life of the first couple, engaging in harassing phone calls.

Throughout the movie, women are mistreated and degraded by men. There are explicit scenes of frontal nudity and smutty references which are not intended to arouse or depict passion, but are simply gross and insulting to the women and the audience.

All of the stars Altman has brought together do fine jobs with very thin material. They may have been willing to do it based on his truly brilliant earlier ensemble films *Nashville* and *The Player*. He may not find it so easy to get them together next time. Mr. Altman, don't forget me. I've done cameos, and everything you do can't be a success. Just ask me.

If this review has bored you, remember that I am saving you from over three hours of boredom and frustration.

Split: Portrait of a Drag Queen (+)

This movie cannot be adequately reviewed: It must be seen to be appreciated. And it's worth seeing. It is the real life story of a young man who, while growing up in the Bronx, recognizes at the age of fourteen his innermost need to cross dress and be seen as a woman.

The film contains what must be home movies of the young boy. He, William, later known as Chrysis (pronounced crises), is a pretty boy who, as he gets older, develops into an even more beautiful woman.

William talks about himself/herself, submitting to the coverage of a camera while he/she walks around his/her apartment telling us of his/her lifestyle. This is followed by scenes on the theater stage where William made his/her living as a drag queen entertainer.

It is extraordinary to see William's breasts. Through the use, more properly described as the abuse, of hormones and surgery he/she developed female breasts while continuing physically as a male with male genitals.

What is remarkable about this film is that it is never crude or prurient. You always have respect, indeed, admiration for this individual who believed he/she had to be himself/herself. There are a dozen friends who are interviewed and speak of him/her almost reverentially, but always with great humor. William died in 1990, at age thirty-nine, of cancer resulting from the breast enlargement.

At one point, we don't know when, William sends a letter to his/her mother, from whom he/she had become estranged. The letter, asking for understanding and signed "your son," is truly poignant.

One of the witnesses in the film, recalling William's youth, speaks of the difficulty such a sexually troubled youth had in a regular high school where he/she was harassed by fellow students. Now, says the witness, the alternative Harvey Milk High School is available. That was created when I was mayor, attacked by many and defended by me. There should be more such schools not only in New York City but other cities as well.

No responsible person will snicker at this movie, but rather will come away respectful of people whose hormonal makeup make it impossible for them to live any other life style than the one that William led. The movie is well worth seeing. Those who enjoyed *Paris Is Burning*—and I did—will enjoy this movie even more.

Stepping Out (+)

Liza Minnelli, as we all know, is a near dead ringer for her mother, Judy Garland, in every way.

Well, déjà vu. *Stepping Out*, Liza Minnelli's new film, is Andy Hardy updated. The plot is just as simple and saccharine, but with brief references to the issues of the day: abortion, incest, unwed mothers and spouse abuse.

Minnelli plays Mavis, a dancer who aspired to Broadway, but never made it. Now she's trying to get a group of dancers in shape for a charity benefit. They are not high school students, but middle-aged, each with a story of his or her own, comparable to *A Chorus Line* or World War II movies.

Minnelli is clearly the star. The rest of the performances are well done cameos, including one by Shelly Winters as the "troupe's" piano player. Many of us can recall Winters as young, svelte and beautiful. Now she reminds us of ourselves: blowzy, double-chinned and heavy.

The real surprise is the marvelous vignette of the only male dancer, Bill Irwin. He goes from klutz to superstar in ten easy lessons. His facial expressions reflect his real life theatrical history as a mime.

Whoever dreamt this pastiche up decided it was going to have something for everyone. It is the kind of movie that won't make you think, and you won't leave the theater humming a tune, but it will leave you with a pleasant buzz.

Footnote: In front of a thousand people, on stage, I once danced a fox trot, the only dance I know, with Liza Minnelli. She was pretty good. I also did a takeoff of *Sugar Babies* with Mickey Rooney at the Inner Circle (New York's Gridiron dinner). Ann Miller, his partner in the show, who was also in our act, warned me, "Watch out for him. He steps on people's lines because of his ego." She didn't know that my ego would protect me—and it did.

The Story of Boys and Girls (−)

In deciding what movie to go to this week, I went through the *New York Times* movie section. In the ad for *The Story of Boys and Girls*, *Times* movie critic Janet Maslin was quoted as saying, "Highly accomplished," so I decided to take a chance.

It's terrible. Avoid it like plaque. Yes, plaque, not plague.

The story is simple and numbingly straightforward. Two families meet for the first time at an engagement dinner for their son and daughter. The boy comes from a wealthy Bolognese family and the girl from a country farm family. There are lots of boys and lots of girls. They are in and out of one another's beds in the course of a single night, as the meal goes on, yet the movie is devoid of sensuality. *The Golden Girls* sitcom is sexier than this movie, except there it's only talk, whereas in this movie, they are in constant boring embrace.

Whatever happened to the earthy Italian movies and stars like Anna Magnani? Either the Italians are keeping their best new movies for themselves or their blood has gone thin—and that's hard to believe.

The Story of Qiu Ju (+)

This movie on modern day life in the Chinese countryside is not for everyone; it is very slow moving. But for those who are interested in seeing China close up, particularly the peasants who make up most of its population of over one billion, the movie is enthralling. With quiet simplicity it provides insights into the minds of those who live in villages under the most difficult of circumstances, only hours from large cities, but eons away from the satisfactions of those urban centers.

The movie opens with a long scene of a thoroughfare in a town filled with people walking or biking, probably returning home at the end of the day. The unending multitude gives us a sense of the enormity of China's population. The camera then focuses on two women pulling a cart on which lies a figure, Qinglia (Liu Pei Qi). We later learn he is husband of one of the women, Qiu Ju (Gong Li), who is very pregnant and clearly uncomfortable doing her share of the carting, and brother to the other woman (Yang Liu Chun). Qinglia has been severely kicked in the groin and is writhing in pain. Who kicked him? The village chief, Wang (Lei Lao Sheng). Why? Because Wang was incensed when Qinglia insulted him by referring to his wife having given birth only to hens—girls.

The doctor to whom Qinglia is brought says he will recover, to the relief of Qiu Ju, who feared that his "plumbing" would be so damaged he would be unable to father more children. Qiu Ju emerges as a woman of indomitable will and courage extraordinaire. She has a sense of what is right and demands that her husband be compensated by the chief. She doesn't want money—she wants an apology.

In fact, this movie might very well have been called "The Apology" for its entire one hour and forty-five minutes is devoted to Qiu Ju's efforts to achieve justice.

Just how Qiu Ju achieves justice will have to await your presence in the theater. Qiu Ju is a beautiful woman. However, her courage and willingness to fight city hall are more important and they make this movie special and worth seeing. She is everyone's best daughter and wife, possessing both strength of character and beauty.

A Stranger Among Us (+)

Melanie Griffith, who stars in this movie as a police officer, has been trashed by other critics. The truth is her part is not actable. No one could have believably played the part of this policewoman who goes undercover to live with what appears to be the Satmar Rebbe and his family. The director, Sidney Lumet, should have realized the New York City Police Department would never send an undercover police woman, with all of the problems attendant to such an arrangement, to live in the Rebbe's house. So understandably her faux pas in dress, speech and sexual enticement of the Rebbe's son, Ariel, are off the wall and would never have happened.

But don't blame Griffith. She did as well as any other actress would have, given the material.

This movie is worth seeing by Jews and non-Jews if only to pique your interest. Regrettably, most members of the Hasidic community will not see it because they don't watch television or go to the movies.

Sidney Lumet, deserves applause for attempting, albeit without total success, to integrate a highly detailed cultural foreground with an action-packed detective story backdrop. Most directors don't have the guts to try non-formula movies.

Strangers in Good Company (+)

Strangers in Good Company is a terrific movie that centers around a group of elderly women who are on a bus trip. One of them suggests a side trip to a summer cottage she used in her youth. The bus breaks down on a rural road leaving the women looking for both the cottage and assistance. At first the women find an abandoned house in need of repair in which they bed down. They later happen upon the cottage they were seeking.

The film works because this is one extraordinary and charming group of ladies. They range in age from seventy to over eighty. Each is different and separately profiled with references to their youth illustrated through earlier photos of them from childhood through midlife.

One of the women is a nun, the most competent of the group, who seeks to repair the bus's motor and actually knowledgeably dismantles the carburetor. Another is a Mohawk Indian grandmother who catches fish for the group to eat.

The oldest person in the group is eighty-three. She appears somewhat prissy at first, but after she admits her age and removes her wig at the urging of one of the women, she becomes very natural. For the first time she seems to accept herself physically. One of the women is an artist who confesses to one of the other women, a garrulous English woman, that she is a lesbian. The English woman is very sympathetic, particularly when the artist tells her that she concealed her sexual orientation for sixty years and now can't stop talking about it.

Strictly Ballroom (+)

This is an absolutely delightful movie that is really an Australian fairytale. If you thought that *Saturday Night Fever* was extraordinary and that John Travolta was a spectacular dancer, whom you envied because of his grace, you'll be delighted with the charm of this film and the grace of Paul Mercurio, who plays the male lead.

The plot is simple, as a fairytale should be. The time is now, give or take a few years. Based on this movie, one would conclude that in Australia there is a dance craze: in this case, not disco, but ballroom. Young men and women practice the different ballroom dances beginning in childhood, hoping to win the prizes awarded at the regional and national dance tournaments.

There are little subplots along the way that take you back to the simple movies of Judy Garland and Mickey Rooney. The music accompanying the dancing is at times so poignant you may shed a tear, as I did, even while thinking; "Why I am I doing this? It's a fairytale." But I've shed tears at other fairytales too: "Pinocchio," "Beauty and the Beast," to name two (the stories not the movies).

When I left the theater with my brother, walking ahead of us was a guy in his thirties who had just exited, and so help me

God he started to do the tango on East 62nd Street and First Avenue. He was not too good; nevertheless I snapped my fingers to keep time and to show my appreciation for his effort. My specialty is still the fox trot, and I'm really good at it.

Terminator 2 (–)

I finally saw *Terminator 2*.

When the original *The Terminator* came out, I didn't go to see it at the movie theater because I thought it would be juvenile drivel. I was pleasantly surprised when I watched it on video one evening with some friends at Gracie Mansion. The film had interesting and fully formed characters that made you concerned for their safety, if they were the good guys, and interested in their fate, if they were the bad guys. I thought it was superbly done and that Arnold Schwarzenegger, whom I hadn't seen before in any movie, was a very good actor.

Indeed, after seeing *The Terminator*, I happened serendipitously to see Arnold Schwarzenegger at Elaine's (a moderately priced restaurant with a continental menu—the Caesar salad and veal chop are good—the restaurant's still chic). I told him what a wonderful job he had done in a uniquely interesting film that was destined to be a model of its genre. He seemed to genuinely enjoy the compliment and appeared not to be taken with himself. He was surprisingly short in stature, well-proportioned, and did not look muscle bound.

Having enjoyed *The Terminator*, I looked forward to seeing *Terminator 2*. If it is true that the producer spent $100 million on this movie because of special effects, it is a sin to have spent so much for so little. There is no question that the special effects were spectacular, but they were repeated over and over again.

There was no character development and no empathy created between the viewer and the figures on the screen: I was indifferent as to whether or not the young boy described as our future leader would be killed in the here and now or would survive to save the world.

Schwarzenegger, playing the good terminator in this film, was in a constant gun battle with his molten-metal enemy, the bad terminator, resulting in: small holes, large holes, but never death by gun shot. Firing at each other from the gitgo clearly was a waste of their time and mine. I found Schwarzenegger's performance somewhat wooden compared to the original .

At one point, there was a dream sequence involving the nuclear destruction of a major U.S. city. I must confess, I hoped all the characters, good and bad, would gather together at ground zero at the moment of the attack: Their being vaporized would have freed me from what I can only describe as exciting tedium.

True Romance (+)

This movie rivals *Reservoir Dogs* in violence, blood, gore and exceptional acting. You either like the genre or you hate it. One of my three companions couldn't take it and left after an hour.

But staying was not a chore for me. I liked the movie, as I did *Reservoir Dogs*. It may be a failing on my part, but I like violence—confined to the movies.

The story is simple and direct. Clarence Worley (Christian Slater) is a young man working in a store which, I think, sells soft porn material. He discusses comic books sold at the store with a young woman, Alabama Whitman (Patricia Arquette), who picks him up in a Kung Fu movie house. It develops that she is a hooker who sought Clarence out because she was hired by his boss as a birthday gift to him.

Alabama is a gamine type, quite beautiful and endearing in her naiveté. She says he is her third trick since she entered the business. They fall in love in those first few hours together, and it is believable.

Clarence then seeks to punish her pimp, Drexl Spivey (Gary Oldman). The scene where he does that, after first being beaten up by Drexl, is terrifying. Oldman does a brilliant job as the pimp, who is also a major drug dealer.

The plot thickens as Clarence—after unintentionally killing the pimp—leaves, taking a suitcase full of cocaine with him, thinking it contains Alabama's clothes. Clarence and Alabama get married and hightail it out of town.

On their way to California they stop off to see Clarence's father, Clifford (Dennis Hopper), a retired cop. Hopper, as always, is brilliant in his role, which has him as the victim of Vincenzo Coccotti (Christopher Walken). Coccotti appears on the scene to reclaim the stolen cocaine for the Mafia family for which Drexl, the pimp, had been working.

Coccotti and his hoods torture Clifford, trying unsuccessfully to get him to reveal where his son has fled. The conversation between the two is not only chilling—Walken being the epitome of evil—but is absolutely the most explicitly racist dialogue you will ever hear. The Mafioso learn of Clarence and Alabama's destination by finding a telephone number on the refrigerator.

Clarence and Alabama are now in L.A. looking to sell their stash to a Hollywood producer, Lee Donowitz (Saul Rubinek). They are introduced to him by his gofer, Elliot Blitzer (Bronson Pinchot). Pinchot's cameo role should earn him an Oscar. Another superb cameo is created by Brad Pitt, an all-American boy in *A River Runs Through It*, and here the epitome of a druggie, constantly stoned and in a fog.

There is a scene of graphic violence in which one of the Sicilian hoods captures Alabama and nearly beats the life out of her. It's painful to behold.

The denouement is hilarious and violent. The police seek to entrap the movie producer on tape by bringing the cocaine to him and having him offer to buy it. They wait in the next room to break in when he makes the necessary admissions needed for arrest. Hilariously, at the same time, the Sicilian mob is waiting to burst into the same room to recapture the cocaine. It all happens almost instantaneously and the number of bullets fired must have equaled a Bosnian firefight as mobsters, cops, and the drug purchaser and his crew are mowed down.

What happens to Clarence and Alabama is a critic's privileged information and provides for a range of emotions on the part of the audience: incredulity, horror, satisfaction. Slater and Arquette turn in powerful performances.

B.B. said, commenting on the violence, "There is no hope if this movie is any reflection on the violence and vile language out on our streets."

M.B. interrupted, "Do you think that people like that really exist?" B.B. said, "Yes, I do." M.B. added jocularly, "I'm close to joining a religious order after seeing all of this violence: but it is well written."

Under Siege (+)

I saw this movie on a plane coming back from Los Angeles. This plane had a personal television set at your seat and a list of videos were made available early on. Having seen almost everything else, I picked *Under Siege*. I had not seen it on the big screen because I was intimidated by the widely held view that Steven Segal is a kind of declassé figure; the cognoscenti wouldn't be caught dead attending his movies. But let me tell you it is a mistake to so judge Segal. He is a very good actor with great style.

The film is a far-fetched adventure flick, one of the genre that a highly acceptable actor, Bruce Willis, had made famous, e.g., *Die Hard* and *Die Hard 2*. Segal is every bit as good in acting and style as Willis. *Under Siege* concerns the hijacking of the Battleship *Missouri* by terrorists led by Tommy Lee Jones who, as always, does an excellent job of acting the role of a bizarre character. The ninety minutes are filled with killings, occasional kinky displays and ultimately the triumph of good over evil. See it on the big screen. It's still around. You'll like it.

Unforgiven (+)

The ecstatic reviews this movie has received, saying it is at the top of the western genre, are vastly overstated. It is good—and certainly worth seeing—but it's not that good.

The star strangely enough is not Clint Eastwood, who does an excellent job playing William Munny, but rather Gene Hackman, who plays the real heavy, Sheriff Little Bill Daggett. The two other stars are Richard Harris and Morgan Freeman. Harris also plays a heavy, but in a much smaller role. He plays an English outlaw who looks like Howard Hughes did at the end of his days, thoroughly unkempt, lacking only Hughes's nearly foot-long toenails and claws. Freeman plays Eastwood's sidekick, Ned Logan.

The movie opens with a bordello scene in which a cowboy goes wild and literally hacks a girl with a knife, disfiguring her face. The other prostitutes, led by the madam who is not an independent contractor but works for the saloon keeper, are so enraged they bring the matter to Sheriff Daggett's attention. Instead of arresting the cowboy and his comrade (a younger man who is remorseful while the older cowboy is not), the sheriff, who is himself a bully and corrupt, tells the culprits that the older cowboy need only give five horses to the saloon keeper pimp, and the younger cowboy two horses, to compensate him for the girl's damaged face. The girl, who is now worthless to the pimp, is to receive nothing.

Incensed, the madam and the girls pool their savings and offer a reward of $1,000 to anyone who kills the two culprits. Enter a young bounty hunter, the Schofield Kid (Jaimz Woolvett) who, knowing he cannot do the killings by himself, solicits Munny to help him. Munny, a widower with two young children who is now a pig farmer, has given up his disreputable life which included murder, mayhem and boozing. But he decides to join the young man and brings along his sidekick from his earlier reprobate days, Ned Logan, a black man married to an Indian woman. It is interesting to note that Morgan Freeman's character is never the subject of any apparent racial discrimination by the sheriff or others. So even though at one point he is severely whipped by the sheriff, there is never a word said conveying racial animosity.

Unforgiven mainly concentrates on the hunt by the three bounty hunters for the two cowboy culprits. Shootouts take place when the two are tracked down and killed. While the film is always interesting, it lacks any sense of urgency. Perhaps that is what other critics see as brilliant, that it is really closer to life in the far west than is normally portrayed, even in the great westerns of John Ford.

The silhouette scenes pictured on the plains as well as the vistas and the town in which much of the action takes place all convey reality. Even when they are breathtakingly beautiful to behold, one never senses that anything is contrived.

Clint Eastwood directed *Unforgiven*. He must be an unusually secure actor and director to have allowed Hackman to dominate the movie as he does and to let Freeman have an equal role. Those of us who remember Clint Eastwood from his earlier days in the television series *Rawhide* will see the ravages of time etched on his face with the passage of perhaps thirty years since he came upon the scene. He is still strikingly handsome with high cheek bones, someone who will look like John Lindsay or a Viking until he dies.

This movie is worth seeing, but it does not set a new standard for westerns. There have been so many more made over the years that are vastly better, with *Stagecoach* and *High Noon* at the top of that list.

Unlawful Entry (+)

This is an especially good detective story and spine tingler. It didn't receive rave reviews from some of the key critics, but I'm telling you to go see it if you like the genre.

A young rising architect Michael Carr (Kurt Russell) and his wife Karen (Madeleine Stowe) are asleep when someone breaks into their home. Hearing the robber, Carr, golf club in hand, goes down to see what's going on. His wife follows and the robber puts a knife to her throat using her as his hostage to get away. The couple is understandably shaken.

Two police officers arrive, Pete Davis (Ray Liotta) and his partner Roy Cole (Roger E. Mosley). The robber is black as is Officer Cole. The criminal in the movie had to be black because there is an important and chilling scene that recalls the Rodney King case; the movie is set in L.A. where the King police brutality incident occurred, so there is a direct parallel.

Officer Davis, magnificently played by Liotta, appears through his looks, intelligence, courage and concern for the victimized couple, to be the ideal cop. But, in fact, he is a rogue cop. He is pathological, a real sickie. For the next hour and a half the movie details his efforts to intrude upon the lives of the couple, who see him as their protector.

The final fifteen minutes, filled with blood and gore, will keep you at the edge of your seat very much like *Fatal Attraction* and *Cape Fear* did.

The acting is truly splendid. Liotta's performance rivals the extraordinary acting he displayed in *GoodFellas* as Mafia hitman Henry Hill. His ruggedly handsome face and distinctive soft spoken voice make him a sympathetic character, albeit in both movies he played a grossly evil person. Madeleine Stowe plays Karen Carr with intelligence and humor, making her quite believable as a loving wife who is interested in her husband's career, while maintaining her own as a teacher. She is willing to confront her husband when she thinks he is wrong in the early hostility he demonstrates towards Officer Davis. That hostility stems from several bizarre incidents that occur when Michael concludes Davis is not what he appears to be.

Roger E. Mosley as Officer Davis's partner accurately portrays the cop buddy system which too often involves protecting one another at any cost, including covering up the other's failures and even corruption. He ultimately breaks the "blue code," but too late.

Utz (+)

This is an unusual film: Existentialist, perhaps, if I can figure out what that really means. You feel the film getting down into your gut—you're not quite understanding it, but liking it anyway. You're never bored, even when the film hardly moves and, worse, eludes rationality.

Utz, based on a novel by Bruce Chatwin, takes place in Prague, Czechoslovakia, when the communists were still in power and it was still one country. Utz (Armin Mueller-Stahl) is Baron Kaspar Joachim von Utz, a collector of Meissen porcelain. We meet him at an auction where he purchases a musician monkey figurine after outbidding an American art dealer, Marius Fischer (Peter Riegert). They strike up a friendship because of their interest in porcelain figurines.

We travel home with Utz and see his collection, which is worth millions. Utz is cared for by Marta (Brenda Fricker), who is his housekeeper and more. We also meet his physician (Paul Scofield).

From then on there are flashbacks to childhood and fantasies of death including images of Utz's funeral. There are interesting vignettes that appear to have nothing to do with the ongoing drama, including one of a lovely young woman who goes skinny-dipping in a lake alone with a goose who seems very affectionate and glides alongside her. A peasant sees them, and believes her to be a witch with the goose as her lover; he goes to arouse the villagers who come back with pitchforks to do her in. She is saved by a passing car that whisks her away. Is this a dream? Is it real? We learn later who she and the driver are.

The communist government confiscates the collection of porcelains, but mercifully allows Utz to retain them until his death; the government agent doing the inventory is the curator (Pauline Melville) of the museum where they will ultimately go. There are many lovely scenes involving Utz and what are described as his two loves: porcelain figurines and women.

There is no sexual excitement attempted—after all, we are witnessing the end of a life. But Utz's graceful dance with a female visitor, too endowed everywhere, is a joy to behold, as is the anger and jealousy of Marta, watching the dance as she washes the dishes.

There is a surprise ending that is both poignant and painful. I liked it, but I don't know why and am not sure you will. It is an unusual film.

Venice/Venice (–)

This film is the brainchild of Henry Jaglom who produced, directed, wrote and starred in it.

As Senator Lloyd Bentsen might have put it, "Henry Jaglom is no Woody Allen."

So, what's it all about, Alfie? Hard to say. But let me try. A film director, Dean (Henry Jaglom), is in Venice at a worldwide film festival. His movie has been selected by the U.S. government as its entry. He is interviewed by the press *ad nauseum*. His constant response to the reporters is that he doesn't understand why he was chosen. He is not, he says, representative of the American movie-making industry. He simply wants to make films by plumbing his own depths and the cores of his actors. He points out he doesn't even tell the actors in advance what their parts are so that they will create from within.

All of this is supposed to convey how deep and different he is. He walks around, as Woody Allen does, with a head covering that resembles an old WWII fatigue hat. Jaglom is revealing himself by parodying Woody Allen, along, of course, with attempting to emulate Allen's introspection. The difference is that Woody Allen is a cinematic genius and what he says, how he says it and what his fellow actors say and how they deliver their lines is interesting, fresh and absorbing, even if the characters are offbeat to a fault and often neurotic.

The title of the film comes from the two cities in which the script unfolds, Venice, Italy, and Venice, California. There are some lovely panoramic views of Venice, Italy. But believe me, if you're interested in visiting or revisiting that lovely city, which I have been to, rent the video *Summertime* with Katherine Hepburn and Rossano Brazzi which is far more captivating. I've never visited Venice, California, and, after this movie, I don't plan to.

Voyager (−)

Voyager is a retelling of the Greek Oedipus myth with the gender roles reversed. In this film, the unknowing father seduces his own daughter, who also is unaware of their true relationship. Sam Shepard, as Faber, is father to Julie Delpy, as Sabeth, a nubile adolescent woman, looking for adventure.

In real life, Sam Shepard is a major playwright, having written, among other plays, *Fool For Love*. He has been praised by other critics for his performances in a variety of films, including his portrayal of Chuck Yeager in *The Right Stuff*. In *Voyager* he is absolutely terrible.

Shepard is now something of a cult figure with the cognoscenti. Based on his performance here, he should stick with writing; he did not author this clinker. The story itself is filled with so many twists and turns, as well as improbabilities and coincidences, that it would be difficult for any actor—no matter how talented—to successfully navigate this misbegotten plot. Delpy is more credible than Shepard, but she still does not cut it.

Nothing in this film is believable. If the tale of incest intrigues you, read the original Greek myth.

White Men Can't Jump (+)

I decided to see this flick because a partner in my law firm who is a serious sports fan told me it was hilarious. I asked him,

"Will I enjoy it even if I don't like baseball?" He did not flinch (knowing I didn't have a better feeling about basketball) and said, "Yes." He was right. It's not a great film, and certainly not in the class of *My Cousin Vinny*, but it does resemble the later because of the way several of the roles are handled, particularly that of Gloria (Rosie Perez). Perez plays the beautiful Puerto Rican woman with a gorgeous accent, street smarts and intelligence who lives with one of the two main characters, a white basketball hustler named Billy (Woody Harrelson).

The locale is a black community in California. After Billy hustles Sidney (Wesley Snipes), a tough-talking playground basketball player who plays pickup games in local school yards for money, Billy and Sidney team up. The way their scam works, Sidney invites others to play him and allows them to select whom his partner will be from those sitting around. As if by accident, but actually by design, Billy is there looking for a pickup game. Naturally, the mark always picks the white guy for Sidney to team with because everyone in the black community knows that, "White men can't jump." Of course, they've never seen me.

The hustle is depicted many times in the film. Surprisingly, it never wears thin because it is accompanied by a superb sound track with a terrific beat and dialogue in black English, 50 percent of which I didn't understand. It made no difference. It was very funny.

The black players are constantly involved in a word game which my brother tells me is called "The Dozens." It involves two guys insulting each other, primarily referring to the sexual activity of the other guy's mother. The winner is whoever comes up with the grossest or most bizarre description of such sexual conduct.

I remember once in Congress being denounced by a friend and member of the Black Congressional Caucus as a motherfucker because we didn't agree on a particular vote. I was so angry that I told him I would never speak to him again. He later took me aside and said, "Ed, motherfucker doesn't mean anything." We resumed our friendship. Let me say it is still strange to hear the putdown game, but I've lightened up over the years and now find it funny. I still don't think I could engage in such a game, so that's just another reason for me not to participate in a pickup basketball game.

The added thread running through the film is that Billy and Gloria are on the run from two bounty hunters for the Mob because Billy owes the Mob money. Another subplot concerns Gloria's desire to become a contestant on "Jeopardy." As a result, she spends a lot of her time memorizing oddball facts. I learned from her that the proper word to describe the object of Adam's temptation offered by Eve was a quince not an apple.

All in all, while the movie is kind of a combination of *Boyz N the Hood* and *My Cousin Vinny*, it doesn't come up to the standard set by either of those. But on its own, *White Men Can't Jump* provides an enjoyable couple of hours.

Wide Sargasso Sea (−)

This movie received an incredibly wonderful review from Vincent Canby. The impression given was that we were in for an erotic visit to the island of Jamaica shortly after the slaves were freed by the British in the 1840s. The story was described as a prequel to *Jane Eyre*: intriguing. The review implied an element of soft porn was present, saying about one of the film's main characters, "her lush beauty and sexual abandon are as intoxicating as the landscape; the film's eroticism is real."

So what went wrong? Everything. The sex was flaccid at best. The director assumed that shots of bodies, black and white, writhing and glistening with sweat accompanied by drums beating in the background, and occasional couplings between the two main characters, Antoinette Cosway (Karina Lombard), and Rochester (Nathaniel Parker), would allow the audience to experience vicarious passion. It failed. Everything was devoid of passion and obviously choreographed. The nudity was discreet and kept to a minimum.

I must confess I don't remember much about *Jane Eyre*, on which the story is based. One exiter from the movie told me, "If you liked Heathcliff, you'll like this." Since that was a reference to *Wuthering Heights*, he doesn't remember his classics either.

The accents are a joke: Some of the former slaves speak flawless American English; some speak with the West Indian English that many of us love to listen to today, as spoken by Geoffrey Holder. Every now and then Rochester has a surreal dream about drowning in the Sargasso Sea—hence the title.

Does it all sound like a mishmash? Well it is and I've just touched on some of the frailties of this movie. It had great potential, but turned out to be a miserable failure.

FIVE

Restaurants, Recipes and Personal Observations

Brazilian Chicken Salad

Courtesy of Sonia, my hosts' (B.M. and D.M.) chef
in the Hamptons
Makes 6 servings.

Ingredients;
   3 chicken breasts sauteed and shredded
   ½ yellow pepper (chopped)
   ½ red pepper (chopped)
   ½ green pepper (chopped)
   1 small can corn

1 small can peas
3 grated carrots
3 hard boiled eggs (chopped)
1 onion (chopped)
juice of 1 lime
½ box golden raisins
½ can crispy potato sticks (shoestring)
salt, olive oil and mayonnaise to taste

Mix all the ingredients together except the mayonnaise, oil and potato sticks. Add those three ingredients just before serving, otherwise the potato sticks will be too soft and lose their crispness.

Choice Hors d'Oeuvres

Every summer I spend several weekends at the summer home of Bobbie and David Margolis and always on Labor Day weekend: We eat, drink, talk and go to the movies. Bobbie was the Commissioner of Protocol in my administration, which brought her into close contact with heads of state and diplomats from all over the world. She has given me her three closely-held family hors d'oeuvre recipes. They are superb during the summer and just as terrific in the winter. They are very inexpensive. If you'd like, you can serve the three of them as a full-course meal. As hors d'oeuvres, these recipes serve between six and eight people.

Zucchini Appetizer

6 baby zucchini, sliced very thin
4 cloves garlic, chopped
½ cup olive oil
salt and pepper
kosher salt

Heat olive oil as for frying potatoes. Fry zucchini in small batches, removing each to drain on absorbent paper while you fry next layer. Using 1/4 cup of the oil in which the zucchini was fried, cook garlic until melted. Put zucchini slices back in pan with the garlic, stirring to heat thoroughly. Place on heated plate and sprinkle with kosher salt before serving.

Maura's Faux Crab Salad

3/4 lb. sea legs supreme (processed hake and pollack available in packages at most supermarkets. It's a Japanese product.)
3 scallions, chopped fine (white and green)
2 sticks celery, chopped
½ lemon
1 tbsp. mayonnaise
1 tbsp. sour cream
salt and pepper

Dice sea legs. Add chopped scallions and celery. Mix together mayonnaise, sour cream and juice of 1/2 lemon. Add to sea leg, scallion and celery mixture. Season to taste with salt and pepper. Serve on toasted pita bread triangles.

Quogue Chicken Wings

3 lbs. chicken wings
salt and pepper
½ cup butter
4–10 tbsps. red hot sauce (Frank's Louisiana or Tabasco)
4 cups corn oil
blue cheese dressing

Cut off wing tips and discard. Cut wings in half (at joint), pat dry and sprinkle with salt and pepper. Melt butter in saucepan and add red hot sauce to desired degree of spiciness. Heat oil to

400 degrees. Add wings, one layer at a time and fry, stirring frequently, for 15-20 minutes. When wings are crisp and brown, remove and drain on brown paper bag. Brush wings on both sides with hot butter mixture and put under preheated broiler in one layer. Broil until butter sizzles (1-2 minutes). Serve wings on warm platter with blue cheese dressing.

Blue Cheese Dressing

½ cup mayonnaise
½ cup sour cream
1 tsp. lime juice
1 tsp. dijon mustard
½ lb. blue cheese (preferably imported)

Mix mayonnaise, sour cream, lime juice and mustard well. Stir in crumbled cheese and refrigerate, covered, for 1 hour.

If you use any of these, let me know how they turn out.

Dinner Party Tips

Now let me give you some tips on how to have a dinner party at your home, inexpensively and successfully.

For hors d'oeuvres, go to Murray's in Greenwich Village at 257 Bleecker St. at the corner of Cornelia. Murray left twenty-five years ago. The store recently relocated across the street from its original location. It's now in a larger space, has a huge selection of foreign cheeses and the prices are good.

You should buy the following: Large Spanish olives (ranging from $2.49 to $4.99 a pound) or oil-cured Moroccan olives ($2.49 a pound) and taramosalata (carp roe caviar) which comes in a jar ($2.99 for the 16 ounce size) and has to be doctored by adding chopped onion to it. The onion costs more than the taramosalata if you use Maui Maui from Hawaii or Vidalia from Georgia, but it is worth it. I mash the onion into the taramosalata in a bowl and then put it all back in the jar to marinate for a day. You can dab it on Bremner wafers ($2.19 a box) or lightly smear the spread on stalks of Chinese cabbage, which you can find at Balduccis or any Korean fruit and vegetable store. Either way, delicious. Do not put salt in the taramosalata, but do add a lot of black pepper.

Another cracker spread that I use is cream cheese with herbs and garlic ($5.99 a pound). The secret extra ingredient is Roland's sun dried tomatoes ($11 for a 15 ounce jar, which should last you for several parties).

Try the cheese sticks. At $10 a pound, a real bargain. And Murray's is also the cheapest place to buy Eli Zabar's sour dough baguettes ($2.00).

I often serve steak as my main course. You should purchase those at the Florence Meat Market located on Jones St. near West 4th. Ask for Tony. The Meat Market has a special cut which only Tony carves called Newport Steak (not to be confused with a Newport roast). The steaks are generally cut in 12-ounce slices and cost about $4 each. They are superb in taste and tenderness, especially served rare.

The best dessert is still ice cream. The cheapest of the well known brands, but equal to gourmet brands, is Breyers. It's available at any supermarket, sometimes for as little as $2.99 a half gallon. My favorite is the combination chocolate and butter pecan. Garnish the ice cream with Nestle's chocolate morsels. Follow up with cordials. I recommend Armagnac. A little more expensive than Calvados, but worth it.

But the real secret to a successful dinner no matter who's cooking—eleven bottles of wine for eight people.

Gail Koch's Mushroom Soup

This soup, which I sampled on Memorial Day weekend, prepared by my sister-in-law, is excellent. If made with skim milk, it is also good for dieters—sorry about the butter, but life is filled with compromises.

Ingredients:
  2 ounces dried Shiitake mushrooms (more if an extra "woody" taste is desired)
  2 pounds portabello mushrooms (or substitute any type)
  2 pounds button mushrooms
  1 stick butter (unsalted)
  1 cup of wine (sweet wine or even tequila)
  64 ounces chicken stock (or make your own)
  1 cup milk (skim milk or half-and-half can be substituted; it depends on how rich you want it)
  2 large onions
  pepper

Soak dried mushrooms in wine about half an hour to an hour. Saute onions in stick of butter until translucent. Clean the mushrooms (not the dried ones) by cutting off the end stems and wiping them off with paper towels. Do not use water. Cut up these mushrooms and put in pot with onions. Let them cook down. When they have cooked add the soaked mushrooms with soaking wine. Cook until they seem almost done. Add the chicken stock and pepper to your liking. Cook about 20 minutes. When broth tastes done, take soup and put the solid part into blender with some liquid and blend until creamy. Keep doing this until all the soup has the same consistency. Put back into original pot. Add milk. The milk will dilute the flavor a bit and make it creamy. It is now ready to be served. Use a cup of mushroom for garnish. Makes more than 12 cups.

Gazpacho

The following is a recipe for the best gazpacho I've ever tasted, prepared and served at the home of Mary and Bruce Barron by Miriam Sanchez.

  4 scallions
  2 large cucumbers
  4 large tomatoes, peeled and de-seeded

2 medium size red peppers
1 teaspoon garlic salt
3 tablespoons olive oil
2 tablespoons red wine vinegar
Worcestershire sauce
Tabasco sauce
salt and pepper
16 oz. can tomato juice

Except for the tomato juice, put everything together in a Cuisinart—adding the Worcestershire, Tabasco, salt and pepper to taste—until pureed. Place in any type dish. Then add the tomato juice. Place in freezer for three hours, stirring once an hour. Remove from freezer and serve.

Serves ten.

Jonathan Thaler's Guiltless Chili (Vegetarian)

From my nephew Jonathan Thaler

2 large eggplants (peeled and diced into 1/4" cubes)
2 green, red, or yellow peppers (cut into matchstick size pieces)
1 large onion (diced)
6 cloves garlic (minced)
1 small hot pepper (minced) optional
2 large cans black beans
2 large cans kidney beans
1 large can peeled stewed tomatoes
1 small can crushed tomatoes
1 small can tomato paste
2 tablespoons chili powder
2 teaspoons cumin
1 teaspoon ground black pepper
1 teaspoon salt (optional)
1 teaspoon red pepper (optional)

together. Smear top and bottom of fish with mixture. Place in heavy duty pan and broil close to heat for 2 minutes. Remove from heat. Remove fish from pan and place on a separate dish. Juice in pan will be used later so do not discard.

Ingredients for sauce:
    6 tablespoons butter
    3 egg yolks
    ¼ cup heavy cream
    ¼ cup very good dry white wine

Melt butter in pan with fish juice. Separately mix yolks, heavy cream and wine together. Then add to fish juice and butter mixture. Cook over low flame until the sauce starts to thicken. If it becomes too thick add more white wine. Take fish by itself and cook under broiler for approximately 7 minutes, checking frequently that it is not overcooking. Pour sauce over fish and serve.

The Weekend Diet

If you are trying to maintain a weight loss, but are experiencing a brief relapse into old habits, I recommend the following for a weekend shock to your system: Farmer cheese ($3.65 a pound at Murray's), sheep yogurt ($1.65 a cup at Balducci's) and a Comise pear ($1.98 a pound at Balducci's). They're best eaten in combination, mixing the three tastes. As far as I know, it's all fat free (maybe) and delicious.

Where To Buy . . .

Shoes

Since 1960, I have been buying my shoes at Lloyd & Haig during their twice yearly sales. At these special sales, in addition to an across-the-board 20 percent reduction on all shoes, they also have discontinued first-class shoes for as much as 50 percent off. In the twelve years that I was mayor, I bought ten pairs of shoes. I still have every pair and they are in very good condition.

When you consider that on sale a pair of shoes costs about $125, and that just to get shoes resoled (full soles and heels) costs at least $30, they are a terrific bargain. (A word to the wise: when you have shoes resoled, never get half soles. They look tacky.) It's important to buy a set of shoe trees (they cost about $20) for every pair and you should change shoes every day of the week, so keep seven pairs if possible. It's a wise investment since they rarely wear out.

Men's clothing

The best bargains in town for long-sleeve regular as well as pullover shirts are available at Brooks Brothers' twice yearly sales. Since their regular prices are quite reasonable, the extra 25 to 35 percent off provides you with phenomenal buys.

The Custom Shop has the best made-to-order shirts in the country, half the price of Turnbull and Asser, and just as well made. Turnbull and Asser may have flashier color combinations, but they're English, so they can get away with it. If the same combos were tried by an American manufacturer, they would be labeled garish. But, somehow, if they have an English label they look terrific.

Gifts

I buy most of my gifts at the Metropolitan Museum of Art. They have several gift shops in the museum itself, as well as stores at the Rockefeller Center promenade, in Macy's balcony and the main branch of the New York Public Library.

They have a wonderful selection of reproductions of ancient jewelry and statues. Any woman receiving an Aztec, Roman,

Greek or Egyptian bracelet or earrings, accompanied by a description telling them exactly where the original was found, will love it.

Another great gift is the Medici horse reproduction, the original of which is now in the Duchy of Liechtenstein collection. I've bought three, two for friends and one for myself. I buy bonded composite reproductions. The bronze replicas are much more costly. Of course, the bronze won't break, but none of my composites have either. In addition, they have a selection of ladies scarves and men's ties and suspenders with ancient patterns, including some from the Napoleonic period available at prices far below comparable merchandise at Gucci.

A Friend's Bar Mitzvah

Normally I go to the movies with friends on Saturday night, but this Saturday I went to celebrate the bar mitzvah of a friend who, at an age close to mine, not having been bar mitzvahed at thirteen, decided he would do so now. What a wonderful event. To be present in the synagogue when he read the required bruchas at the reading of the Torah, followed in the evening by dinner at a superb restaurant, was a unique evening and far better than being at the best movie.

As I saw him standing at the altar, it brought back memories of my bar mitzvah so long ago. He, as I, displayed nervousness, sure we would forget our part in the service, occasionally hyperventilating. But he didn't miss a line, nor had I. My eyes felt moist as I listened to his bar mitzvah speech and remembered mine.

At one's bar mitzvah you accept the responsibilities of adulthood, or as we used to say, "Now I am a man." We, for good reason, don't use that sexist terminology any more, and women are now bas mitzvahed. He, my wonderful friend, knew his rite of passage, which is what a bar mitzvah is, had to be fulfilled nearly sixty years later. The rabbi held the Torah scroll over his head saying, "This is the law. It can be summed up in one sentence. Do nothing hateful to another which thou would not have done to thee. All the rest is commentary." What a film it would have made.

Restaurant Reviews

Baci

Baci, at 412 Amsterdam Ave. between 79th and 80th Sts., which I hadn't been to before, has good inexpensive Italian food. The pastas are delicious.

Cafe Greco

Prix fixe restaurants are springing up all over the East Side. Last week when my sister asked me to join her and other members of my family for dinner at 6:15, I thought, "A bit early, but okay if that's what time she wants to meet." When I arrived, I understood why. In order to be eligible for the early-bird dinner, all orders must be placed by 6:20. Given that for $14.95 the early bird dinner includes an appetizer, entree, dessert and beverage, it's worth the early start.

For an appetizer I had octopus. Others in my party had soup and salad and all were superb. The entrees include salmon, tuna, lamb chops, steak and much more. I had three double lamb chops (the regular portion) and they were delicious. The rest of my party were also pleased with their choices. For dessert, while tempted by the pies available, I thought about calories and instead had the fresh fruit which was a huge portion and delicious.

In addition to excellent food, the ambiance at Cafe Greco is lovely. It is located on Second Ave. between 71st and 72nd Streets. There are lots of well-polished brass rails and two different levels in the dining room. If you don't want to rush to arrive by 6:20, an even larger menu is available later on for $19.95.

Chinese Restaurants of Choice

Now I'll tell you about a few of the restaurants that I frequent with pleasure. I'm not reviewing the ones I don't like, because I don't want to add to their problems. And in fairness I would need to go back several times and find them consistently bad, to rate them as such. I never go back a second time.

There are three Chinese restaurants I think are as good as the best in the city but at one-third the cost of the more expensive midtown joints. A first-rate dinner at any of these three restaurants should cost no more than $15.

Try the **Peking Duck House** at 22 Mott St. Order the duck, eggplant with garlic, sizzling beef, Chinese fried flounder, string beans with shredded pork. Close with fried bananas and walnuts—an extraordinary dessert. Order family style and insist that they bring one dish at a time. Order at least one dish for each person in the party, but count the Peking duck as two. Ordering this way makes for variety—remember, at least four dishes for a good dinner. A Peking duck for just two people requires two world-class appetites.

Across the street at 13 Mott, is **Sun Lok Kee**, which is the best place for seafood. (Ambience be damned!) The specialties are steamed Canadian oysters in black bean sauce (the oysters are as big as golf balls), fried chicken (it's called fried, but it's really roasted), mussels in wine, sizzling octopus or sizzling scungilli. Prices are modest, as is the seating arrangement.

Then heading uptown, there's **Ollie's** at 2315 Broadway at 84th St. The menu is extensive and excellent. The scallion pancakes are particularly good.

At the Peking Duck House and Sun Lok Kee, if you are in doubt as to what to order just say, "The Mayor sent me. I'd like to eat what he eats." Then quickly add, "I mean the old Mayor, not the new Mayor." At Ollie's they hardly know me. After all, it is the radical upper West Side, and they threw me out—politically, that is.

Da Umberto

Da Umberto, at 107 W. 17th St. between Sixth and Seventh Aves., still has the largest menu selection in town. Good food at the reasonably high end. I like their veal cutlet with arugula salad on top.

Downtown Restaurant Picks

While at City Hall, there were three restaurants that I frequented:

River Run at 176 Franklin St. between Hudson and Greenwich Streets is the most reasonable. Their best dish is the fish of the day. Ask for hot garlic and oil sauce to pour over the fish. (Of course, only if you are a garlic freak like me.) They also have very cheap and delicious diet salads (ask for a double order of the house salad, and it's still under $5) and, for those not diet conscious, Mississippi mud pie.

The Odeon at 145 West Broadway between Worth and Duane Streets is elegant, reverse chic. Its basic decor is "cafeteria," which is what it once was. I go there for lunch and occasionally for dinner on weekends. The menu is continental, and everything is well prepared. I always order the country salad, ofttimes as an entree under $10. The calamari appetizer is also superb. They have stopped serving their wonderful sour dough baguettes—big mistake on their part. A restaurant can make or lose its reputation on the bread it serves.

The Bridge Cafe at 279 Water St. is a small, old bar-type restaurant, under the Brooklyn Bridge, a little off the beaten track. When I was mayor, I often had lunch there and the food was consistently delicious. Their sauteed salmon with garlic was the best in town.

Gage & Tollner

Brooklyn, (718) 875-5181

This is the oldest restaurant in New York, with a landmark interior including gas lights. It's owned by a friend of mine, Peter Aschkenasy, but this review is objective. The wonderful chef, Edna Lewis, specializes in Southern cooking. The menu is huge, with a large variety of seafood dishes, and the prices are moderate, ranging from $10 to $20 for lunch or dinner. If you are looking for a low-calorie meal, try the turnip soup. If you team it with a dozen cherrystone oysters, you have a delicious, nearly fat-free meal. If dieting isn't your concern, then try the Charleston She Crab soup and the swordfish—delish. The restaurant has its own free parking lot, a big plus in this town.

Gotham Bar & Grill

Not long ago, Molly O'Neill, food critic extraordinaire for the the *New York Times* and much more, reviewed the **Gotham Bar and Grill** (12 E. 12th St.) dinner menu and gave it three stars. She mentioned that it had a prix fixe luncheon menu for $19.93, so I decided to go.

Everything that Molly wrote about the restaurant in such glowing terms was right on target, and to have it available for $19.93 made it a bargain. It was obvious from her review that Molly enjoyed her quite costly dinner and I enjoyed my, as my father would have said, "cheap as borscht" lunch.

Hatsuhana

While it has a Park Avenue address, this restaurant has its entrance on E. 46th St. in a pedestrian mall. The restaurant is simple, tastefully decorated, and the food is excellent. On top of all that, it's cheap. For $15.50 you can have a filling lunch which includes soup, salad, and any of half a dozen entrees. My three favorites are chicken teriyaki, salmon teriyaki and the chicken and sushi combination. Dessert is extra. Since I like to avoid fat, I don't eat their delicious ice cream. (You ask: how do I know it's delicious? On occasion, I have taken a taste from someone else's.) I always have the pineapple, which is ripe and sweet. Lunch reservations are necessary because the place is always crowded.

Jewel of India

My usual choices of restaurant cuisine are Italian, Chinese, and Japanese. If you are watching your weight—and I always am—you can maintain strict dietary controls with any of the above, but particularly with Japanese. However, if you know what to order with the others, you can also limit your caloric intake without suffering.

I like Indian food, but I don't have it often because almost every dish is loaded with calories and swimming in delicious oil. You spell oil O-I-L. I spell it F-A-T. But it's fat that makes most meals really delicious.

I recently went to **Jewel of India**, located at 15 W. 44th St., for their special buffet lunch. At $10.95, it's an outstanding bargain. First, you serve yourself a delicious salad: lettuce, onions, cucumbers, herbs and yogurt dressing. Then a choice of any or all of about seven entrees. On the day that I was there they included tandoori chicken, lamb bhuna and chicken jalfrezi, but the menu changes from day to day. I had a little of everything and a lot of lamb and bhartha (eggplant). The latter was the best.

The buffet lunch is on the second floor of the restaurant. The special does not include dessert or coffee, but if you have dessert—and they are light and delicious—with tax and tip your bill should be around $21. There is a lovely ambiance and the service of the waiters in removing the dishes and silverware and bringing the dessert and coffee to the table is excellent.

You can also have lunch or dinner downstairs with a much begger menu, but it will cost more. I've done it and it's worth it.

Old Homestead

I recently returned to the **Old Homestead Steak House** at 56 Ninth Ave., which I haven't been to for maybe thirty years. I went because H.K., who had gone at the suggestion of J.R., a meat maven involved in the wholesale meat distribution business, said that it had the best roast beef in New York City.

So I went, and it is absolutely true. For $29.95, they give you a two-and-a-half pound prime rib that is the best I have ever had. It was so large that for the first time I can recall I had to ask for a doggy bag. I had decided that I couldn't possibly allow the excess meat to be thrown away and that I would give it to the first homeless person I saw on my way home. Would you believe that I did not see a single homeless person between 15th St. and Ninth Ave. and 8th St. and Fifth Ave. on a Saturday night?

So, I took it upstairs and put it in the refrigerator, knowing that I wouldn't eat it because I only eat red meat once a week. On Sunday morning, I brought the one-pound slab of beef still on the bone, which is the best part, to H.K., who was in the hospital having a knee joint repaired. His eyes lit up.

I think I shortened his hospital stay. During the week I brought him a combination corned beef and pastrami sandwich from the Carnegie Deli. It cost $9.75. As good as the sandwich was, the prime rib was a better buy.

Park Avalon

This large bistro, which serves lunch and dinner as well as Sunday brunch, is always crowded. I have been there several times, and it is inexpensive with good food and large portions. As a devotee of salads, I can tell you their chopped salad with feta cheese, roasted peppers, tomatoes, cucumbers and fresh basil at $6.95 is the best I have had anywhere. Their lunch and dinner menus include a wide variety of pizzas as well as meat and fish entrees; a selection of sandwiches priced from $7.50 to $10.95 are available at lunch. Dinner entrees range from $12 to $18. They also have an excellent dessert menu. The place holds several hundred diners and gets a Madison Avenue crowd ranging in age from 20 to 69. I know the upper limit from personal experience. It is located at 225 Park Ave. So.

The Swing Street Cafe

The Swing Street Cafe at 253 E. 52nd St. is a very small but unique restaurant. At lunch, appetizers are about $5 and pasta entrees are under $10. The pasta pesto is my personal favorite.

Tartine

A wonderful new cafe has opened in Greenwich Village: **Tartine**, at the corner of W. 4th and W. 11th St. Yes, they intersect, off Seventh Ave. Their prices are phenomenally cheap. Brunch at $6.95 includes fresh orange juice. Eggs Benedict and coffee, as well as other choices. The pastries are superb and baked on the premises. Dinner is an even more astounding buy. Delicious grilled salmon for $8.50, equal to any I've had elsewhere for as much as $22. The only drawback is that it has only about ten tables and only one that seats five, but don't let that stop you. It's owned and operated by two young Frenchmen, Thierry Rochard and Jean-Francois Benard. It has a take out service. Their full size cakes sell for about half of what you pay at Dean & DeLuca.

Piccolo Venezia

This is a superb Italian restaurant located at 42-01 28th Ave. in Astoria, Queens. The portions are huge. The prices are moderate to high and the food is spectacular. It is worth traveling to. Seafood and pasta are their specialties.

Siam Inn

I found a very charming, inexpensive Thai restaurant in mid-town, the **Siam Inn** at 916 Eighth Ave., between 54th and 55th Streets. There were four of us and we ate like there was no tomorrow, turning the customary Siamese personal style of dining into a Chinese restaurant kind of feast—everyone sharing everything.

At our request the waitress did the ordering and she did very well. We had two orders of mixed appetizers, each $8.95. And then we had four orders—beef, chicken, pork and fish. The total bill, including superb Thai beer, came to $20 a head. Well worth it.

Sign of the Dove

Some of the best bargains in town are the prix fixe lunches offered at many restaurants throughout the city. **Sign of the Dove** (Third Ave. at 65th Street), probably the most beautiful restaurant in town, has one of the best. Their prix fixe menu is offered Tuesday through Friday from 12:30 until 2 p.m. For $19.94 you can choose from two items for an appetizer, an entree and a dessert; it excludes beverages (e.g. coffee), tax and gratuity. While it is more than you may normally spend for lunch, it is well worth it.

Thai House and Bubbys

There are two cafes that I recommend in TriBeCa. One is **Thai House Cafe** at 151 Hudson Street on the corner of Hubert Street (right outside the Holland tunnel). The chef is extremely accommodating to make certain that the spicing is to your taste, and the prices are modest.

Appetizers are $6, meat and seafood specialties range from $8 to $10 and vegetarian dishes are $6.

For dessert, walk two blocks south to a place where all the locals eat: **Bubbys** at 20 Hudson Street. It has an ambiance similar to down-and-out cafes in Amsterdam. I only had cappucino, which was delicious, but B.S. had a slice of three-berry pie which he obviously found scrumptious. The selection of pies includes apple, banana, pecan and chocolate and are about $3.50 a slice.

Triangolo

Triangolo, a new restaurant at 345 East 83rd Street, has the look of a small trattoria in Rome: simple alfresco along with an attractive room and very inexpensive. My nephew, J.T., goes there regularly and brought it to my attention. The menu is simple, but adequate. The appetizers range from $5.50 to $6.75. We had among us arugula salad, mussels and seafood salad, all excellent. The majority of the pastas run about $9.50. I had spaghetti sauteed with marinated plum tomatoes, basil and garlic for $8.50. It was excellent. They accept no credit cards. Reservations are absolutely required because the lines are long.

West Street Grill

Litchfield, CT, (201) 567-3885

The proprietor of this charming restaurant located at 43 West St. in Litchfield, Ct, is Jim O'Shea, a young Irishman who still has his brogue. Start with their grilled peasant breads. I have the recipe for their Parmesan aioli with fresh herbs. I swore never to give it out, and I won't, but it's delicious. I had the soft-shell crabs at $19.95. Their desserts are exceptional. The best was mocha creme brulées. Reservations are necessary for weekends.